DREAM TO RISE

FROM DARKNESS INTO LIGHT

CYNTHIA ENCINAS-CONCORDIA

ISBN: 978-1-960136-33-6

Table of Contents

INTRODUCTION

What would you love to do, to have, to be, to create, and to give? Each one of us has had an experience in life wherein we have reached rock bottom, gotten stuck, and felt scared to move in order to swim back to the surface of the ocean. Are we waiting passively, allowing this to happen, or do we choose to work our way through it in order to find and reach that light?

Waiting may not be the best way to achieve our goal. We need to put in the work for that light to manifest, and that is when wonderful things in our lives begin to work their way into existence. We are in control of what and who we want to become. We have the power to create what we want in life. And what is it that we want? Those are our dreams. The dreams that we have been hoping and praying for in order to reach a more meaningful life.

I have experienced a lot of challenges and failures in my life which caused significant stress, and at one point even led to depression, which surely enough, impacted my relationship with my husband, children, other family members, friends, and even the people I meet on a daily basis. Besides transferring my negative energy to them, my physical health began to deteriorate. I was always feeling anxious. I experienced fear of interacting with people and felt like I had no drive to keep on living.

Take a second to think about whether or not you have felt the same way or experienced something similar. We do not deserve this kind of life. It is so easy to get caught up in the mindset that tells us that "we can't do it," "it's too much work," "it can't happen to me." But the truth will always be...YES, you can! The only one stopping you is YOU. You can have that abundant life that you want. You can break past those barriers that keep you frozen in fear and thinking that things will "always be this way."

Life is a learning experience. Each interaction with every individual and situation contributes to what we become, whether it's how we perceive life, how we view challenges and failures, how we become visionaries for our own purposes, or, most especially, how we are able to impact others' lives and contribute to creating a better world. Life is a blessing that allows us to experience God's love through others and His creations. Life is not just about seeking achievements and accomplishments. We need to experience challenges and failures as well—that is the exciting part about being alive and living life to the fullest.

My Journey Made Me

In this book, a diverse range of amazing authors will share how they have gone through their traumas, how they were able to fight such battles, transformed, and are now living the life they love.

This is the main reason I started my business, Dream to Rise LLC, last September 2020.

I believe that a lot of you might also be stuck in your own dark bubbles (as I was). I hope our stories will inspire you and give you even just a spark of hope that there truly is light at the end of the tunnel. It has been my dream to write an anthology book because I know we can help change lives across the world. After all, if we were able to manifest our dreams, then so can you. I don't want you to miss the enjoyment that life has to offer. Life is great!

Cynthia Encinas Concordia

Dream to Rise LLC

https://www.linkedin.com/in/cynthia-concordia-2b51b8116/
https://facebook.com/cynthia.concordia
https://www.instagram.com/cynthiaconcordia
www.dreamtorise.info
www.youtube.com/@cynthiaconcordia8346

Cynthia Encinas Concordia is a transformational life coach, published author, podcaster, motivational speaker, mother, and grandma.

As a Human Resource practitioner at the World Bank (retired, Headquarters, Washington, DC) her job involved dealing with diverse groups of people. This professional knowledge, experience, and skillset coupled with her personal life journey led her to share and work with others to create the life they would like to live.

"I had the best opportunity through my life journey, to see the value of making a positive impact on others' lives. I felt a calling to make a difference by inspiring others and creating awareness to empower people to unlock their full potential and create a life they love. I am results-oriented and passionate about personal growth and mindset mastery.

With me fulfilling my purpose, I am now leaving my footprints so the young generation may be inspired and continue what we are doing – making an impact in this world.

Join me on this incredible journey of self-discovery and let's create the life you've always dreamed of.

I want you to live your dreams and welcome each day full of gratitude, saying, 'Life is great!'"

Cynthia is the proud founder of Dream to Rise LLC. Her books include *My Journey Into Becoming*, *Overcoming Self-Sabotage*, and the *Dream to Rise* anthology.

HOW CAN DARKNESS SPREAD LIGHT TO OTHERS?

By Cynthia Encinas Concordia

Introduction

Have you created a dream? A very expansive dream?

Now, have you made your dream a reality? I am sure a lot of you would say "no" to this question. You would say that your dream is still in your fantasy world. Why?

Most of us create our dreams by default. We are constricted by the circumstances and conditions surrounding us. We are still affected by our past pains, traumas, fears, limiting beliefs, news we hear on TV, wars, inflation, etc. See the baggage we have been carrying? That's the reason why it is hard for us to move forward in manifesting our dreams.

A lot of us are stuck in our dark bubble for quite some time and can't move forward. Are you overwhelmed by negative comments that are making it difficult for you to make decisions for yourself? These thoughts have been running in my mind for most of my married life. I was afraid that I might be judged, rejected, or afraid to make mistakes.

You may have reached your rock bottom and don't know where to go. Darkness just enveloped you and you're wondering what life really is about.

What is rock bottom? According to the Merriam-Webster Dictionary, it is "being at the lowest."

Hitting rock bottom is one of the most unpleasant experiences in life. When you are at the lowest point in your life, you get bombarded by all sorts of unpleasant emotions—fear, insecurity, doubt, frustration, hopelessness, and depression.

However, it was because of the challenges that I went through that I became the person I am right now. I have viewed life from a different perspective. Now, I see life as an adventure, a journey that lets you experience successes and failures. You may have your ups and downs, but the most important thing is how you view each one. Do you view your downs as threats or punishments or as opportunities?

I would like to share with you my life's journey and how I overcame challenges and reaped achievements, which led me to become a transformational life coach—not just for me, but for my family as well, most especially for my children, Nathalia (32 years old), married to RJ and a mother to her baby girl (8 months old), and Gabriel (27 years old). It will explain why and how I became the Cynthia that you know. What brought about the new Cynthia?

Each one of us has a light to share with others. The only problem is we tend to keep them to ourselves because we are still determining how others would perceive them. We have that fear, doubt, and worry overpowering our light.

When I experienced my struggles leading to rock bottom, I asked myself, what would happen to me if I stayed there? What will my life be? Will I be living my life to the fullest? Definitely not! During that time, I had to decide whether to choose light or stay in darkness.

Life Story: Problem

I was married for 23 years and blessed with two children. My marriage was a roller coaster ride. I was subjected to domestic violence, which started when my daughter was only five months old back home in the Philippines. Like many immigrant families, we moved to the USA to provide our children with better opportunities, as well as to work on our marriage. However, instead of working towards the marriage that I had aspired for, things turned out much differently. By 2011, my late husband was on two restraining orders (the first in 2005 for 72 hours and the second in 2011 for two years). During those two years, I remember constantly telling my children that their father loved them so much. I did not want their relationship with their father to break. I believe that, as humans, we all make mistakes and deserve second chances. And so, I was exhilarated when my children invited him to each of their high school and college graduations.

The worst part came four months after their graduation when he died due to massive cardiac arrest. I remember crying so hard when I saw him in the emergency room because there was still so much conflict to work through, not only in our marriage but also with our whole family. I felt we still had a lot of work to do to get to a place of forgiveness—a place that I now felt like we could not reach because he was gone.

For six long and agonizing years, I felt nothing but guilt. I stayed in my own dark world, stopped interacting with my friends, became depressed, and ultimately allowed this to impact my physical, mental, and emotional well-being. I had a huge fear of being judged and rejected by others, especially our mutual friends and his family members. Some of those friends and families even stopped communicating with me and our children after his death. Only my relationship with God kept me going during those dark days of despair. He was my source of strength, hope, and light.

When I got to the point where I felt life was no longer worth living, my son shared with me that he wanted to go to the *Culinary Institute of America (CIA)* for a Culinary Arts and Food Studies degree. I had completely forgotten that I still had my son, who needed to attend college! By then, I was a single parent, and so came the next worry—how would I be able to afford it? That was the moment when my perspective shifted: I could not keep allowing the past to decide my future; I had my son's dreams to think about! This new perspective motivated me to ensure that I not only provided for my son but would also work on myself in the process.

My focus was not just to ensure that he got to attend his school of choice but that he also thrived in and graduated from that school. With this newfound motivation and passion, I also started giving myself attention and putting myself on the priority list of people to care about. I worked out every day and ate healthy and nutritious food. I later found out that taking care of my health and well-being helped to boost my confidence, which led to a healthier relationship with my children and my family. I discovered that my positive behavior was mirrored back to me by the people I interacted with. This allowed me to focus more on other areas in my life, like work.

Gabriel's graduation at CIA.
Left to right: Cynthia, Gabriel, and Nathalia

With this newfound confidence, perseverance, and change in perspective, manifestation just overflowed. I was promoted, which increased my salary so significantly as to allow even more blessings into my life. Not only that—God connected me with people who gave me advice and insight into downsizing my living situation, which cut 50% off my mortgage. Then, I looked into applying for grants and scholarships. Can you believe I only paid 20% of my son's first-year tuition? You would not believe all the blessings that continuously came pouring in. By God's overwhelming grace, not only did my son finish his college debt-free, but our little family even had extra money to travel to Barcelona to celebrate his success.

Results: Blessings Overflowing

Can you see how the Lord worked in my life? He did not give me the money itself but sent me connections or people who gave me advice, insight, ideas, and gifts. The Lord took care of my problems.

The Lord showered me with the blessings I needed to manifest my dream. The struggles and pains I experienced made me realize that these are a necessary part of my life's journey toward becoming a new and better person. I became stronger, smarter, more creative, and more resilient. I don't believe that the effect of challenges should be to put us down, to stay stuck in our dark bubble, and live a miserable life. Rather, its effect on us should be that we see the chance to make a change, to pick ourselves up, to find out what our character is and where our strengths lie, and to provide a chance to move forward until we see the light at the end of every tunnel. Remember, we cannot see the beauty of gold without going through the fire. Before the glorious sunrise of Easter Sunday is the darkness of the Lenten season.

Due to my life experiences, I have discovered my WHY, which led me to become a life coach—to help and inspire people to realize that they have the power to manifest their dreams and live the kind of life they love. If I could overcome my challenges and turn the hurdles into stepping stones toward a better future, I am sure that others will be able to do it as well.

Because of what my children and I have gone through, they have discovered their strengths and weaknesses, what they're passionate about, and how they can positively impact other people. I am glad they started early.

My daughter, Nathalia, continues to serve as a volunteer firefighter (for eight years) with her husband, RJ. Why? It was a volunteer firefighter who helped revive her dad while driving him to the nearby hospital. Now, she wants to give back by being one, saving lives. On top of her volunteer work, she works as a project manager in one of the government contracting firms.

Nathalia (3rd from left), her husband RJ (2nd from left)
and her co-firefighters in Dale City, Virginia

Gabriel has been passionate about food for so long, which is why he chose to major in Culinary Arts and Applied Food Studies. He likes to travel and enjoys the beauty of nature; he loves to keep discovering what it is that he would really love to be, to have, to create, and to become. He loves connecting with people, learning their culture, and seeing how he can impact them through food. His experience working in restaurants around the world, as well as farming in the U.S.A., inspired him to do more by educating children and parents about the importance of knowing where their food comes from.

Now, as he takes another role at Brigaid in Fresno, CA, he believes that institutions play a massive role in our country's food system in all realms, from agriculture to workforce development. Being a Brigaid Chef will give him the opportunity to help empower the next generation by working with institutions to elevate the children's school meals, advocating not only for sustainability in how our food is produced, but for the people working in our food system as well.

Gabriel, Brigaid Chef in Fresno, California

Cherished moment with Gabriel, RJ, Nathalia, and their bundle of joy.

Being a mom of two beautiful and inspired children, I came to learn and realize that we should not get stuck in our past experiences, in how we were raised, in the paradigms, in our fears, in the feeling that we are undeserving, and in other limiting beliefs that have been blocking us to move forward towards our dream.

We can create our own dreams by design in a more expansive way. We can live in abundance if we want to. The only limits in our lives are those we impose on ourselves. We are in control of our own lives.

When you believe in yourself and in what you are capable of and then take action to work on it, you'll be surprised by how much more you can do to make a difference in and for the world.

It was through my darkness I found the light and now sharing and spreading that light to others. Let us always be that light for others so that others may also spread their light for those who need it.

You won't be able to appreciate the light if you have not gone through the darkness.

How do I remain in my power and continue what I do?

It is my purpose. This keeps me on fire and focused on where I am going. When I created my dream by design and tested my dream, I knew I would be living the life that was prepared for me by God. He is using me as His instrument to spread love and compassion wherever I go. My vision is to spread sunshine and happiness to the people I meet so this may create a ripple effect. I want peace, kindness, compassion, and love to prevail here on earth.

Again, this then led me to become a life coach, write my book (*My Journey Into Becoming*), create a mastermind group to help each and every member of the community manifest their dreams, and launch my podcast so my messages and the stories of my guest speakers will inspire others so later on they could also be a light warrior themselves.

On top of that, I have also volunteered as a Rotarian at the Rotary Club Pasay EDSA back home in the Philippines to see how I can serve my Filipino brothers who live in poverty.

I also volunteer at Family Services in Fairfax County, Virginia to mentor a 10-year-old child who has been abused by her father.

Gifts Derived from My Challenges

What I appreciate from what I have gone through in life is that:

- I interrupted the history of domestic abuse within my family and am now leaving a legacy for not only my children and grandchildren but also for the people we meet on a daily basis.

- I am now a stronger, improved, creative, resilient, assertive, resourceful, and compassionate person because I am spreading love.

- Now, I'm committed to living my purpose to be a blessing for somebody.

- Now, I'm committed to helping others be the best version of themselves.

- Now, I'm committed and passionate about teaching people that they have the true power within them to live the life they love.

Secrets That Will Impact Your Life

For me, the only secret that will impact our lives is this: We CAN live our lives to the fullest! Even with limited time and resources, we have the power to create our dreams and live the life we love. How?

1. Know our "why" or purpose. When we know our mission in life, this will be our living guide. All our plans and actions will be geared toward our dream or mission.

2. Take risks and learn to face fear. If we stay within our comfort zone, we will not discover the opportunities in store for us. Learning is part of growth. When we challenge ourselves, we thrive. Believe in yourself and enjoy the journey!

3. Be grateful for all that we have. When we are grateful, we feel fuller, freer, and more abundant. We now focus on the positive in every situation.

4. Learn to forgive. Remember, forgiveness is about us. When we free ourselves from resentment, anger, and pain we are able to let go of the past, get wisdom from our experience, and move forward.

5. Surround yourself with people who believe in you. We need someone who will support us even if everyone else says our dream is impossible.

6. Be a leader, ready to help, that promotes happiness, support, love, compassion, and peace. Have the courage, take that challenge, and make the change!

Once you see life as an adventure, everything changes. The possibilities and opportunities that reveal themselves in front of you are endless. Enjoy the thrill and allow yourself to fail because that's how you will grow and thrive. It is amazing how your view of the world and life will change.

Alison Lines

Alison's Soul Image
Coach

https://https://www.linkedin.com/in/alison-lines-mba
https://www.facebook.com/profile.php?id=100012376906736
https://www.instagram.com/stylelovedreams
www.alisonssoulimage.com

Inspiring entrepreneur, empowerment coach, certified stylist and image consultant, MBA Graduate, member of the National Society of Leadership and Success and alumni of Sigma Kappa Delta Pi. The beach is my happy place, arts and culture are my jam, and friends and family are my World. Stylist by heart and passionate about empowering women to elevate and reinvent themselves through self-discovery and personal image creation. My philosophy is "Style is not just what you wear, but who you are." ANL.

With a diverse background in many industries, she has a plethora of knowledge, experience and skills, which have helped her to tap into her unique ability to understand others on a highly intuitive level, alongside her Empathic abilities, which are both a blessing and a curse. Her past experiences, knowledge, and her own life traumas have led her to fulfill her purpose of being a soul and heart centered coach.

UNSPINNING THE TOXIC WEB

By Alison Lines

Life Story:

According to the Merriam-Webster Dictionary, toxicity is defined as: "the quality, state or relative degree of being poisonous." What many people do not recognize is that this includes the human race, and in my experience, they are the most poisonous of all and can often spin their web without you ever noticing. This is my story of how toxicity spun its web all around me and how I unspun the web that I had been wrapped up in for over two decades.

Pain:

I suffered for over 20 years from toxicity in my life, especially in my relationships with others. Toxic energy followed me like my shadow and affected my life negatively. Most of the abuse came from the hands of verbally abusive, controlling, and manipulative men as well as others who felt that being in control of me and my life was the answer to their own serious issues. I also was a chronic people pleaser and a born Empath. I was married and divorced twice, sexually assaulted twice in college, and was forced into various unhealthy/risky situations. When my second ex-husband tried to kill me, it became crystal clear my life needed to change! Everything I did was wrong, and I was always being portrayed as a selfish, spoiled brat. Apparently, in their mind, because I was an only child, I deserved to have those titles.

But that is not where my story begins; I experienced forms of control and manipulation starting when I was growing up as the only child in a very traditional and protective family. I grew up with parents who exuded support and love, but at the cost of agreeing with what they value and believe to be true within the world. Being an only child, I was always searching for their approval and often felt shame and guilt if I said no or disagreed with them. At the time, I did not realize that this was my problem and not theirs—they were just responding to me in the only way they knew how.

Throughout my life, I have suffered from depression and anxiety due to overwhelming stress from major transitions, life changes, and situations that made me feel like I was completely backed against the wall with no possible way out. The reality is that there is always a way out. A huge factor was my inability to see my self-worth and to fully discover what makes me unique and God-given gift and purpose on this planet. I would rely on limiting beliefs and past patterns. I would indulge my ego. I had a serious lack of confidence, could not say NO, and boundaries…well they simply did not exist in my world. At this time, I was unable to surrender to God, the Creator, the Universe's ultimate plan and path for me. But, despite everything, I always knew and felt that deep down in my soul I was meant for more, meant for an extraordinary life. I could see visions of all my desires and dreams coming true, even grander than the dreams that I had previously dreamt, for I knew I was meant to change lives, make a global impact, and leave a legacy of epic proportions in my wake. So, what did I do, you might ask? I became a Phoenix that rises from the ashes.

Evolution:

I believe these three words embody who I am: Passionate, Empathetic, and Resilient. Why? Because I am passionate about life and in everything I do, I understand and connect with people through their emotional state, and I never give up, no matter how challenging my situation is. They say your evolution begins when you hit rock bottom, so what happens when you hit it more than once but continue to rise and survive? Eventually, you become so resilient that no matter how many times you get knocked down, you dust yourself off and get back up. But this is no easy task, and it is not for the faint of heart because this is the part where you discover what you are made of. How tough is your mind? Will you let your ego win? How thick is your skin? Will you stop hiding your gift? I found out my skin was thicker and my mind more powerful than most of the people that I was surrounded by. Often, they were shocked to see just how quickly I would bounce back from any given challenge in my life even when the odds were almost impossible, but I have and always will find a way. Whether it be divorce, loss of job, financial struggles, potential eviction, backstabbing friendships, abusive relationships, controlling parents, loss of life, etc. I have been through them all and I have survived. I believe this is one of my gifts—to be able to show others just how easy life can be and that if I survived, they can too. I don't know about you, but I never had a goal of simply surviving. That is thinking small; we are in the business of thinking big. So here, survival is not what we strive for, rather we thrive. If I can have my dream life, so can they, and if I can work through my past demons, they can do the same. It all has to do with your mindset, attitude, the way you treat others, and how you live your life. I believe that I experienced the challenges in my life because God, the Universe, and the Creator knew that I could handle it while others could not. The weight was put on my shoulder so I could lead them from the darkness and into the light, help them become resourceful and resilient, and renew belief in who they are and what they are capable of.

My lightbulb moment occurred when I was curled up in the fetal position in my bathroom fearing for my life. In the blink of an eye, I saw my life flash before me as my ex-husband, who had severe mental health disorders, was standing outside the door walking around with a bloody knife. He had cut himself and was pacing our living room dripping blood from his arm. Earlier, I had told him that I would not end my friendship with one of my best girlfriends; this had been an ongoing point of contention in our relationship and marriage. He had taken so much from me already that I refused to lose another person close to me. This time, I knew that I was done and I was not going to give him that power over me. In hindsight, this was a very dangerous situation that I had found myself in. At the time he told me that if I did not end my friendship, I would have chosen her over him. And that was never allowed. You did not say no to him because you just never knew what his reaction would be.

I walked on eggshells, basically living in a nightmare, for over a year. According to his thought process, I did not love him, and he was going to punish both of us by ending our lives. I remember feeling so much fear and pain in response to all of the trauma he had caused in my life. I thought to myself, is this the end? No, it simply couldn't be. I had called his mom and also my parents and remained in the bathroom while the police were called and put in place outside my apartment building. I remember shaking so much as tears rolled down my face. I knew I had to get out of my apartment and away from him for my safety. I had suffered so much at his hands, and I would not lose another thing to him, including my own life. Luckily, he was being distracted by his mother and I was able to be on the phone with the police. He tried to engage with me, but I was only focusing on what the police were saying. I remember the policeman's voice saying to me, "Walk down the stairs, do not look back, even if he follows you; keep walking down the steps until you get outside to safety. We are right outside the door." As I walked down those stairs, it became clear to me how much my life needed to change and that no one would ever take my power from me again. I said a prayer to God in that pivotal moment, that if I could just make it down these steps, I would change my life and help others do the same. God listened to my prayer, and I am fulfilling that mission with my life's purpose of helping women elevate and reinvent themselves through self-discovery and image creation. I took the most horrifying moment in my life and turned it into something beautiful and impacting for society.

Progress:

The transformation to progress did not happen overnight, just like Rome was not built in a day. It takes time to discover who you are after having your soul kept secret because a man controls your very existence. For two decades, I had lost my identity, and when I decided I was done, I did not know who I was or how I could move forward with my life. I had been dependent on people most of my life, and now that was no more. It's scary, not knowing who you are or your true purpose in life. As I saw the horror fade and watched my World slowly come back into focus, what I realized was this was not the end of life as I knew it, rather it was the beginning of a new journey and a new me. I reinvented the person that I once was by investing in myself and truly digging deep to my core, reflecting on my past, and rediscovering my identity. It started through very small steps, like going back to my psychologist for regular sessions, redefining what I wanted and what I didn't, what I enjoyed doing, and what I would rather not do. I discovered new interests and hobbies and began to bring back some passions that had been suppressed. I invested in a self-love program and a variety of coaches that ultimately catapulted me to truly see what was missing in my life, and a big piece was that I did not love myself the way I should. Another big piece was fun. Apparently, control takes away your ability to be free and have fun. I created a daily routine and practiced meditation, journaling, and my new favorite thing to do, dancing in the kitchen. Slowly, after about a year or so, things began to change, and I became more confident. It is a true process and it took lots of courage and strength to evaluate my life and myself as an individual. During this critical time in my life, I discovered who I was deep down in my soul and started saying yes to what I loved as well as no to what I didn't. I said yes to those who served me and no to those who didn't. It is an epiphany of sorts when you realize who your true tribe is and you kick out all those who are not part of your tribe anymore. Suddenly, you feel as though a major weight has been lifted off your shoulders and you can breathe again.

I started to really envision what I desired in this lifetime and took action to make it happen. Here is what I know: you must get comfortable with the uncomfortable, and that thing that you are good at? It's your gift that you were given by God to share with the World. I always knew that style was my passion. I loved experimenting with outfits and helping my friends pick the perfect look from their wardrobes. I always received compliments from people when I was out and about. I still do. Style was that one thing that no matter what I was struggling with, made me feel at home. Putting on a beautiful dress, or picking the perfect accessories, always made me feel confident, like I could take on the World. So, what is my gift? Well, I have many, but helping people and utilizing style to create the very essence of who they are in this world, thus creating change and impact, is my calling. My philosophy is, "Style is not just what you wear, but who you are." -Alison Nicole Lines

What changed? My mindset. My energy. Where focus goes and energy flows. I am an alumnus of Sigma Kappa Delta Pi Sorority, and a member of The National Society of Leadership and Success. I have pursued my love of acting and participated and been cast in multiple performances and reels. I received my MBA in 2022 and my GCert marketing in 2022, experiencing making people's dreams come true as an event coordinator at Grounds for Sculpture. I officially opened my business in 2022. I am an empowerment coach and certified image consultant. I am currently taking certification courses to become a Life Coach. I am a promoter, ambassador, and influencer for various companies. I was selected and chosen to be in a 40 over 40 photography campaign featuring inspiring female entrepreneurs, recently was asked to be part of a She Rises Studios book anthology as a co-author, and received an award for being a Woman on Fire through a global networking group (which will also include a podcast and international magazine spot). I have also recently participated in multiple podcasts and am quickly growing my presence and authority on social media—all that love of being on camera really paid off in the end.

Fast forward to the present day. I went from surviving to thriving and learned some incredible lessons that I utilize to this day as an empowerment coach and image consultant. My mission is to provide heart and soul—centered, intuitive guidance to empower women who struggle with toxicity to find peace and to work through their pain, forgive, and move toward the best version of themselves to live their very best lives. The biggest epiphany I had was in trusting myself and my intuition, as well as learning how to receive and believe in the true power of gratitude. It is one thing to believe in something, it is another to live it. Every day I embody my purpose and every day I get tested, whether it be positive or negative. Life is a journey, and that journey starts and ends with you. Only you have the power to change your story. Recently, a coach made a very powerful statement, and she said, "I am the One." As I reflected upon my life, I realized what she meant. No matter what we go through in our lives, the trials and the triumphs, we go through them as the One. And the only thing that we cannot be in this life is not the One. So, I ask you, why would you waste such a precious gift as being the One?

Today, I live life on my terms, and I am truly happy. I am building a business to help women and make an impact on this World. I have received many opportunities along my journey and continue to receive them often. I am truly grateful and believe that God, the Creator, and the Universe have created a beautiful path for all of us. Life is beautiful, but sometimes, it is truly a challenge. How does the saying go? "What doesn't kill you, makes you stronger." Once you embrace who you are, and what your purpose is, the World becomes your oyster, and the possibilities are endless. Those challenges that have been holding you back, now seem to drift away into the background, creating a life that only dreams are made of.

The End or The Beginning?

Alison Schnoes

Owner of Growth Pathways Coaching and Courses LLC

https://www.linkedin.com/in/alisonhall/
https://www.facebook.com/GrowthPathwaysCoachingCourses
https://www.instagram.com/growthpathwayscoachingcourses/
https://www.growthpathwayscoachingandcourses.com/

Alison, the owner of Growth Pathways Coaching and Courses, is on a mission to empower individuals to reach their full potential. With a B.A. in Music from CSU-Pueblo, she brings a unique perspective to coaching and personal development. Through being immersed in The Mindset Coach Training Academy by Laurie Burrows, among other programs, she's honing her skills to provide transformative experiences.

Her coaching philosophy centers on individualized approaches, tailoring strategies to each person's unique needs. Alison's commitment to lifelong learning and passion for helping others sets her apart. She firmly believes that everyone can lead their best life.

When not guiding clients, Alison enjoys quality time with her husband, Paul, and their two furry companions, Elsa and Kiowa. Embark on a fulfilling journey with Alison as your coach to unlock your true potential.

RISING ABOVE: MY JOURNEY THROUGH LIFE'S CHALLENGES

By Alison Schnoes

You have read about many fantastic stories of those who have risen against life's challenges and barriers. But here is mine... I am nervous, scared, and stubborn but also different, unique, and ambitious.

Being vulnerable to sharing my story causes nervousness and fear. I had originally told the publisher not to include me in this book. But I changed my mind as my story may inspire you, open your eyes to a different point of view on life, and prove that you can overcome anything that you put your mind to.

I am not from a rich family. We spent most of my years growing up in the working middle class. My mom was a teacher for many years and worked her way up to being a principal. Her dad was a mechanic and her mom was a secretary. My dad was a pastor for 16 years but got burned out, pivoted into running his digital marketing business, and then returned to being a pastor. His parents were divorced, so his grandparents raised him. His grandpa was a leader in the military and could put up a Christmas tree with one index finger. I also didn't marry into a rich family as my husband's parents are also in the working middle class. My parents always taught me to work for what I want and live below my means.

I was born almost two months early, weighing under four pounds. My mom was sick when she had me, and I had to fight for my life in the ICU. Thanks to the doctors partnering with my parents, I survived and later thrived.

Since I was born early, this came with the cost of having a physical disability and developmental challenges. I have Cerebral Palsy, a mild and non-progressive case. I was officially diagnosed when I was nine years old. My main challenges are stiff legs, tremors, and the English language.

I took my first step when I was one year and three weeks old, and then I learned how to crawl on all fours 1.5 weeks later since I preferred to army crawl instead. Ain't that backward? But walking is sometimes still a challenge as my ankle pops out due to the leg muscles tightening and causing pain. Some things that help are moving my legs similar to riding a bicycle and stretching. Due to having the pain of stiff legs, I've never been fond of exercising but I can be motivated as I play Pokemon Go, watch Netflix while riding a stationary bike, and track the number of steps I take per day.

Tremors in my hands happened frequently but learning how to play piano and saxophone helped the muscles and nerves learn how to function better. Now it only happens when I experience the emotions of anger, upset, and/or frustration.

I said "dada" when I was five months old, it took until I was almost eight months old to make many word-like sounds, and I didn't use many sentences until I was four years old. I said "mama" for the first time when I was 13.5 months old. I remember going to speech therapy and leaving school for it even though I had to make up over three hours of English homework for missing class as a third grader. As speaking, reading, and writing are related, all of them have always been a challenge. Yet, I still attempted the junior and senior AP English classes, writing this chapter, and speaking with people daily. Give things a try—maybe they will work and maybe they won't, but you will not know unless you try. If they don't work, you know another way it doesn't and are one step closer to success.

In school, I have always been that different and unique kid. I was a loner who had only one or two friends in each grade level. Friends range in their worth, so I'd rather have four "quarter friends" backing me than 100 pennies.

I attended six schools between Kindergarten and senior year of high school in three different cities. After the private school at the end of 4th grade wasn't a good fit for me due to the lack of accommodations that I needed to become successful in school, my parents moved me back to public schools for the rest of my K-12 education career. At the end of my junior year, my high school was closed due to the building not being used efficiently, declining enrollment, and budget constraints of the district. I changed school districts so that the previous school district could receive fewer tax dollars. In terms of moving cities, this happened in Kindergarten through 2nd grade, 3rd through 6th grade, and 7th through 12th grade. We moved during this time because my dad got a different job.

I learned to pick friends carefully, adapt to change, and face unknown obstacles due to not being in the same group of kids while in K-12. I needed to pick my friends carefully as rejection was already the norm for me but it still hurt nonetheless. When you pick your friends, you are letting them into your life. Your life includes your dreams, desires, and needs, and they can help you create a present and future that you might not like, so you need to choose carefully. Adapting to change is never easy when the world is changing constantly, so moving and growing up taught me to not be attached to one place as home. Home is where I decide to make it. How do you face the unknown? You can believe in yourself, break it down into bite-sized pieces, ask for help and wisdom, and explore a new world for yourself.

I was one of the last kids picked for anything, especially sports. Sports are still the primary way to gather kids together in a group. I encourage parents to explore other options so that non-athletic kids don't get bullied for not having any friends and/or being different. I didn't find a clique to join until middle school band. I started playing saxophone in 5th grade in Kansas. Later, I went to college for music education, and my primary instrument was the saxophone in Colorado.

I had an IEP (Individual Education Plan) for about nine years. I qualified due to my Cerebral Palsy, which is considered a physical disability. My team involved specialists like speech pathologists and neurologists, parents, and teachers. I got to participate in those meetings which taught me to become an advocate for myself. My IEP ensured access under the law to receive additional instruction and accommodations for me to be more successful in the classroom. My additional support included a scribe, access to computers, extra time, and more breaks.

I had to go take an MRI in 7th grade and the machine was loud, but I had to try to stay still. Listening to music didn't work as I was singing to the music. We joke because it proves that I have a brain. I took another MRI about 14 years later, and the Tech asked after the MRI why I was there and why it was ordered. I explained that it was to reconfirm with a new neurologist that I have Cerebral Palsy. My new neurologist was able to confirm using that MRI.

I graduated from an IEP to a 504 in high school which lets schools still help me with accommodations and prepare me for college. I chose not to take my 504 to college with me. The only employer that I have had so far that has asked for evidence of my disability was Walmart. A 504 protects me from being discriminated against due to my disability.

I went straight from high school into college to study music education; being a middle school band director was my Plan A. I took my first flight ever to North Carolina to be a camp counselor for the Eastern Music Festival while preparing for my senior recital. The Eastern Music Festival was very eye-opening to the hard work that bleeds into our lives and I had a great time being a woodwind tech for a marching band another summer. I completed junior and senior saxophone recitals. I played saxophone, oboe, English horn, clarinet, and flute in college ensembles, and all but the flute were featured in my recitals. Thank you to my parents for paying for my music degree.

As a Music Education major, I was required to do student teaching. My cooperating teacher was rarely in the classroom with me so I was alone with between 20 to 60 middle school band students without guidance and support. Despite studying with my cooperating teacher and knowing the assistant principal and the principal, the time came to have a meeting with my college about a different placement to an elementary school at the recommendation of my college evaluator. I learned during the meeting with my college that I had these choices: retake student teaching in the fall in a different placement as I wouldn't become a licensed teacher due to reasons unknown to me as there was no communication from my cooperating school, or graduate with a B.A. in Music. I learned the connections that I thought would not fail me when I needed their help did, so I graduated with a Bachelor of Arts in Music in 2018 and went into the workforce unsure and undecided of my future.

I had to create my next plan, but I was already working as a demo assistant for Music and Arts, and my boss also thought it was odd that the topic of the meeting changed drastically without my prior knowledge as I was progressing properly according to my college evaluations. I also worked as a substitute para primarily in SSN (Significant Support Needs) in a middle school where they tried to convince me to become a special education teacher. It was truly exhausting mentally and physically so it wasn't sustainable as a career.

Sales gets a bad rap but you are selling yourself to everyone you meet, so I sold myself as an employee to a store manager at Guitar Center and started as a sales associate. I didn't know much about guitars, pro audio, or drums when I started, but I achieved training in those areas of the store. I exceeded my performance metrics within one year, including having a month of 10 credit card apps and over 40% with the Pro Coverage warranty regularly. Yet my hours were cut in half, so I had to move on to take care of my family.

I moved to Walmart where I participated in Live Better U which aims to help associates earn a debt-free college degree and advance their careers. I learned that a degree in Business Management and Leadership with a focus on Walmart isn't what I wanted to do. I looked for resources to help me, like text-to-speech apps, and was able to do the required readings which took about 20 hours a week. Coming from the kid who struggled with reading until 5th grade so much that my brother had all of the books memorized, I feel accomplished with how far I have come in my reading skills. During that time, I was diagnosed with hypothyroidism caused by Hashimoto's thyroiditis and sleep apnea which is why I felt super tired all of the time even after four cups of coffee. I don't drink caffeine very much anymore because this could have been caught sooner.

I decided I had enough of working in retail and started looking for jobs at the school district. I applied to become an online community advocate and got it. I work with teachers as a team to re-engage and keep students engaged. My primary role is to re-engage students who are in truancy court or lacking in attendance. I have been there since January 2021, the longest I have kept a job so far in life as I am in my late 20s.

But there is more to life than working just a job or jobs, so I stumbled upon an Instructional Design and Development program. A mindset coaching certification program found me through Facebook since I coach and mentor students as my job unofficially. I created Growth Pathways Coaching and Courses to use my skill sets and my way to help people.

Despite my early challenges with learning, I am now a lifelong learner and I dabble in everything that catches my eye. This currently includes but is not limited to Notary, Loans, Certified Financial Planning, Insurance, Email Marketing, Digital Marketing, Cybersecurity, Data Science, Freelance, Sales, and Voice Acting. I am probably a multipotentialite and am a specialist in some subjects. A multipotentialite is someone who studies multiple disciplinary studies and is probably an interdisciplinary generalist. Always be willing to learn; you will find the door to your dream life. So what are you curious about? Go learn more about that NOW!

Brett Shuttleworth

Founder of Smiling Soul Creations

https://www.facebook.com/TheBrettShuttleworthShow
https://www.instagram.com/brettshuttleworth/
www.smilingsoulcreations.com
https://www.youtube.com/@BrettShuttleworth

Brett Shuttleworth, 'master of the free,' inspires us to journey towards the boundless horizons of our inner selves through self-discovery. As the visionary and transformative force behind Smiling Soul Creations, a multifaceted platform encompassing transformational retreats, coaching academies, and mentorship programs, he has touched over 27,000 lives worldwide.

Brett's journey catapulted him from humble beginnings in rural South Africa to scaling summits as a professional sportsman, gracing runways as a supermodel, captivating audiences as a Hollywood actor, and charting the waters of entrepreneurship.

Today, Brett is a renowned spiritual facilitator fostering personal growth, inner healing, and spiritual awakening.

His mission: creating a ripple effect of love that empowers others to embrace their potential fully. Rooted in love, compassion, and joy, his teachings resonate profoundly with those seeking authentic transformation.

Brett's expanded vision includes Smiling Soul Island Estate in Bali, aimed at individuals seeking a conscious, prosperous, and spiritually enriched lifestyle.

MASTER OF THE FREE

By Brett Shuttleworth

From Homeless to High Fashion: My Journey of Redemption

My name is Brett Shuttleworth, and I have a story to tell—a story of incredible highs and devastating lows. A journey that took me from the dusty streets of a small farming town in Kwazulu-Natal, South Africa to the dazzling runways of New York City's high fashion world. It's a story of redemption, resilience, and the extraordinary power of the human spirit.

My story is not just about a farm boy turned supermodel; it's about a soul's quest for self-discovery, love, and meaning in a world filled with unexpected twists and turns. It's a reminder that even in the darkest of times, there's a glimmer of hope, and the smallest shifts, when nurtured with dedication, can lead to quantum leaps of transformation. My life is a testament to the fact that the human spirit is capable of transcending adversity, rewriting destinies, and, ultimately, the most important goal in life is to find out who we truly are.

A Humble Beginning

I grew up in a small town in South Africa where life was far from glamorous. My father was a charismatic man but steeped in alcoholism. My mother had been swept off her feet by his Elvis Presley good looks and became pregnant with me at seventeen. We struggled financially and emotionally as a result of the chaos of my father's addiction.

My mother left my father when I was seven years old and re-married a man with staunch values, but who was also an old-school disciplinarian. My childhood was spent on my step-father's farm where I learned the value of hard work imposed with a hardness that was often too harsh for my young spirit.

From the moment I could walk, I was captivated by the world of sports. The dream of becoming a rugby star burned more deeply in my heart after my parent's divorce. I needed to prove my lovability and worthiness. As a means to navigate life's difficulties, I poured my blood, sweat, and tears into the sport, determined to make a name for myself.

Shattered Dreams

I was blessed with a sports scholarship that took me to America. I was well on my way to achieving my childhood dream of playing in the Rugby World Cup when a devastating injury shattered my arm into twenty-seven pieces. I was left feeling adrift in a sea of uncertainty, stranded in a foreign country, having to find a new path forward.

The City of Dreams

Determined to reinvent myself, I set my sights on a new horizon—the world of modelling, which I was accidentally introduced to by a friend. With nothing but a dream and the clothes on my back, I made my way to the bustling streets of New York City to test out the waters after being offered an interview with a top modelling agency. Along with being a city of dreams, it could also be unforgiving to those who dared to chase them, as it turned out for me.

I faced rejection often, eventually ending up homeless, living on the streets of the city that never sleeps. It was a humbling and scary experience that tested the limits of my determination, spirit, and courage to keep going and forged my character.

A Guardian Angel

Amidst the chaos of homelessness, I encountered an eccentric figure named Rosario Angelo. He appeared in my life like an angel, offering me shelter and solace beneath the concrete canopy of New York City.

It was the end of a tough day of wandering through the streets of downtown Manhattan, and while I was scared to witness Rosario's eccentricity at first, I succumbed to his offer to help and shelter me as I had no other choice at this point.

Rosario was a janitor whose kindness, compassion, and wisdom were unconventional. He became a lifeline for me in my troubled state. Once I overcame the fear of sitting in a concrete basement surrounded by rats at night and relaxed in my new abode, we shared stories and laughter. Rosario taught me that even in the darkest of times, the power of love and resilience could prevail.

During one of these turbulent times, Rosario offered me this insight which I'll never forget and have since tattooed onto my arm: "Never underestimate the power of denial." It became my mantra—a reminder that I could defy the odds and rewrite my destiny. The Universe's intelligence is always guiding us and aligning our trajectory to a bigger vision we have not considered yet. Have faith when setbacks happen.

Rising from the Ashes

I slowly clawed my way back from the brink with a deeper soul connection and sense of gratitude.

I re-directed my outlook to look for ways to enhance my situation and not let it own me. Through one of these encounters with an agent, I had my big break! Suddenly, I was jet-setting across the globe, walking the world's most prestigious runways, becoming the face of a Ralph Lauren campaign, and picking up work from the world's top fashion labels.

Walking in the Dark Side

The world of high fashion was a whirlwind of glamour and excess. It was a place where appearances mattered more than anything else, and where the pressure to conform to impossible standards was relentless.

One day I needed to be thin, while another client wanted bulky, and a third wanted long hair. It was a constant chase that I had to navigate, which I did with Rosario's teachings in mind, always remembering the importance of staying true to myself.

It is said that all polarity co-exists at the same time. I found this to be true: the glitz and glamour of the fashion world had attached with it an equally dark side. The relentless pursuit of fame and fortune led me down a dangerous path. I partied with the Russian mafia, found myself entangled in scandals, and succumbed to the temptations of sex and drugs. It was a hedonistic lifestyle that threatened to consume me entirely with no gain or benefit for my soul.

A Wake-Up Call

One fateful morning, I woke up in a nondescript motel room next to a fan. I looked at myself in the mirror, and for the first time, I saw the emptiness in my eyes with no joy being reflected back.

There was no satisfaction in my heart despite all the external achievements and status I had gained. I didn't recognise the person staring back at me in the mirror. I didn't even know the name of the woman lying next to me in bed.

I felt nauseated at myself and who I had become through the pursuit of external gratification. It was a deep wake-up call from my soul that I could no longer ignore.

Student For Life

I left behind the glitz of the American Dream and embarked on a soul-searching journey to discover my true purpose in life. I travelled through four countries. Traveling through Greece, I found solace in the simplicity of life, reconnected with my inner truth, and became a student for life.

Birth Of My Daughter

I returned to South Africa and established my own business with the underlying intention to relay a message through a lifestyle brand: Courage Lifestyle and Clothing.

I met a beautiful woman and was gifted with one of life's greatest blessings, which also turned out to be one of the greatest opportunities to expand my heart—I became a father to an angel and found the love of my life through my baby girl, Noa Sunshine! Until that point, I had no idea what it was like to truly surrender to love.

I wanted to sustain my small family's livelihood but most importantly, to be the best Daddy in the world!

I became a Corporate Sales Director of a major company and inspired my team to reach new heights… but life had more challenges in store.

The Battle for Noa

The challenge came in the form of a heart—wrenching breakup with my partner which led to a legal custody battle for my daughter, Noa. I fought hard in the courts but ultimately lost custody to her mother.

It shattered my heart into a million pieces, leaving me broken and searching for deeper answers.

The Quest for Self — Discovery

Determined to find a cure for my underlying pain—exacerbated through separation from my daughter, I trained as a consciousness coach and embarked on a deeper spiritual quest, seeking the answers that would alleviate the suffering.

A Journey of Love and Transformation

As I landed in India, the land of spirituality and ancient wisdom, I felt a sense of anticipation like never before. The air was thick with the scent of incense, and the vibrant colours of India's diverse culture surrounded me. It was a stark contrast to the concrete jungle of New York City, and I couldn't help but be entranced by the energy of the place.

The Land of Serenity, Sages, and Seekers — Rishikesh

My journey led me to Rishikesh, a serene town nestled in the foothills of the mighty Himalayas where the sacred Ganges River flowed gracefully. I checked into the Great Ganga Ashram, a humble abode amidst the tranquil mountains, alongside my friend Bert. I felt an inexplicable connection to this place as if my soul had found its true home.

Meeting the Guru — Bringing Lightness Through Humour!

Our purpose for being in Rishikesh was to interview the most advanced spiritual souls alive on the planet today intending of filming our documentary, 'What Makes Your Soul Smile', while exposing love and oneness. The caveat was we had no money and were doing the whole project based on energy exchange—including the travels!

Filming the documentary led us to the head guru of the ashram, a colourful Italian with an entourage of devoted female monks. In his presence, I felt a sense of lightness, and I couldn't resist the urge to make myself comfortable on his couch. This sparked laughter and camaraderie between us and broke the ice for others too. I had always had an uncanny ability to infuse love into any situation while challenging the norm!

We managed to gain entry to a yoga festival by audaciously printing our logo and 'FILM CREW' on T-shirts despite not having the expensive entry passes. Soon, even the gurus themselves sought interviews with us.

Love Awakened

As I interviewed spiritual leaders and wandered the vibrant streets of Rishikesh, I felt an overwhelming sense of love. It flowed through me like the sacred Ganges itself. I observed the chaos and harmony of India, realising that a nation with such a vast population and diverse challenges could only thrive through love.

India's chaos and enthusiasm inspired me, much like New York always did. I felt a calling to fully embrace the unknown and share the love I had discovered with the world.

Living Your Passion

My journey in Rishikesh also led me to dine with Janet Atwood, co-author of the New York Times Best-selling book *The Passion Test* and a figure in the book documentary *The Secret*. Our conversation touched on passion, commitment, and came from a place of love for the benefit of all.

Later, I savoured coffee with Bert and Rupali. Rupali was going through a divorce and had joined me and Bert while we filed the documentary. We ended up having a spontaneous, music-filled evening with no alcohol and vegetarian food. I marvelled at the beauty, serenity, and freedom in the air, induced not by alcohol but by the joy and simplicity of life.

Gurmukh Kaur Khaksa — The Yoga Rockstar

I had the honour of interviewing Gurmukh Kaur Khaksa, a 68-year-old yoga instructor with a worldwide following. Her unique teaching style was akin to a rock concert, and her radiant presence left an indelible mark on me.

When asked what made her soul smile, she replied, "Serving others and showing gratitude." Her life's work and her ability to spread joy through yoga inspired me to further understand the power of love and service.

Love as the Ultimate Wisdom

Throughout my journey, I interviewed numerous spiritual leaders and discovered a common thread: Love.

I came to understand that living from a place of love was the ultimate wisdom. Love meant living in alignment for the benefit of the whole, not just myself, but for everything and everyone.

I realised that anyone could be a teacher, an angel, or a guru. The source of wisdom and inspiration could be found in the simplest acts of love and kindness, from a garden boy to a spiritual legend.

As I enjoyed my last cup of chai in Rishikesh, a moment of profound realisation washed over me. Staring down a narrow alley, I felt a oneness with the world, understanding that every decision made out of love aligns us with the universe's purpose—to create heaven on earth.

My journey in Rishikesh was a testament to the power of love, service, and gratitude. It was a reminder that, in the pursuit of wisdom, we often find the answers in the most unexpected places, and that the greatest journey is the one that leads us to our own hearts.

The Colours of Love and Power of Unity

In the heart of bustling Delhi, a city teeming with life and chaos, I found myself on another remarkable adventure. It was a road trip through the vibrant streets of India's capital alongside my exuberant soul sister, Rupali, who could turn any moment into a carnival of laughter or trip over herself!

The Jama Masjid, a magnificent mosque in the middle of Old Delhi, reminded me of the unity that can exist even amongst people from different walks of life, coming together in prayer and harmony. It was a vivid lesson in the importance of embracing and celebrating our differences while recognising the common thread that unites us all—love.

The Power of Love's Ripple Effect

My journey through India was a testament to the transformative power of love. It was a reminder that love was not confined to romantic relationships but could be expressed in countless ways—through acts of kindness, service to others, and a deep connection to the world around us.

My journey had come full circle. I had witnessed the many colours of love. It was a journey that had changed me profoundly, and I knew that my mission was clear: to share the message of love and its transformative power with the world.

Master of the Free

I teach this message today to people on my Smiling Soul Retreats based on the journey I took and journaled about. We have expanded our Retreats to include Bali and South Africa. I have founded a company based on love, Smiling Soul Creations, which includes a Smiling Soul Coach Training Academy, Mentorship Programs, and an online community of like-minded souls who get together to remind themselves that that which you seek is also seeking you—and it is love, the ultimate success. All you have to do is stop listening to the self-sabotaging thoughts that tell you otherwise!

Put in place methods such as attending a spiritual retreat, taking a course, or engaging in activities you love to keep yourself aware of the miracle of love that is present in each moment within you! I invite you to come on in—the water's beautiful!

I have recently expanded my vision to include Smiling Soul Bali Island Estate. It's a dream that—like the retreats—will unfold in its time. But the most precious gift is available to each of us now—and that is love as our true nature. To live from this awareness is to be truly free!

Namaste

Cheriess Maree

Accelerated Excellence
Life Coach, Hypnotherapist, Author

https://www.facebook.com/profile.php?id=100090617543470
www.accelerated-excellence.com
www.acceleratedexcellence.com
www.recipeofawarrior.com
www.wieldedbyawarrior.com

Hypnotherapist, Certified Life Coach, Guided Meditation, Six Phase Reframe Instructor, Fiction & Non-Fiction Author, Wife, Mom, Survivor, and Warrior of Peace.

My past experiences have only given me the tools needed to understand, relate, empathize, and become the voice for those who have none. I am the Warrior who wields the sword of peace, breaking the cycle of abuse and violence, coaching, helping, and inspiring women!

My skills in hypnotherapy have helped break addictions, build confidence, and lessen the effects of emotional triggers from the past. Addressing the roadblocks of the mind with Hypnotherapy, combined with the support of a coach, visualization of Six Phase Reframe, and

Guided Meditation can make for a smoother, more successful, path for your future.

I feel a great sense of peace and accomplishment when I know I have made even the slightest difference in someone's life.

Sincerely ~ Cheriess Maree

FORGED IN FIRE

By Cheriess Maree

"With a heavy hand the iron is beaten, shaped, and dipped in flames, only to become a magnificent weapon of peace wielded by a Warrior."—Cheriess Maree

"No truer words could describe the journey I have endured, emerging from the flames like a sword, my intuition and purpose have become sharpened and powerful, as an instrument of peace, yet wielded by a warrior." ~ *'Recipe of a Warrior' by Cheriess Maree*

†

I stood there in the kitchen trying to understand my mother's sudden change in behavior. She had started crying while making the macaroni and cheese lunch for my little brother and me. I watched her fall to her knees as she began hitting the floor with her fist. Then she crawled under the kitchen table, curled up into a ball, and started sucking her thumb.

This was the moment my entire life took a huge turn. I was barely six years old, watching my own mother transform into a helpless baby.

†

The passing of time is foreign to a child. I couldn't tell you if it was three days or five. All I knew was that I had watched my favorite morning cartoon at least three times! We were running out of Coco Puffs cereal and grape juice, which all the three of us had eaten for the past few days. I was not allowed to operate the stove, so I fed my little brother and the stranger under the table what I could find.

And yes, when I say stranger that was exactly what she was. The lady under the table was no longer my mother, but a scared little girl sucking her thumb and peeing her pants.

That evening I crawled under the table with her and offered the only comforting thing I knew. I began brushing my fingers through her hair, remembering my mother had done this to comfort me.

✝

The phone rang… I had never actually answered the phone before. It was on the wall near the kitchen. I quickly pushed the kitchen chair over to the wall and climbed up to answer the phone.

"Hello?"

"Cheriess? Honey, is that you?"

"Hi Granny!" I exclaimed.

"You are so grown up answering the phone!" She mused at me. "Put your mamma on the phone dear."

"She isn't here," I answered truthfully.

"What? Is your daddy there?"

"Nope, he is still in Alaska…"

"Cheriess, honey, your mamma isn't in the house? Is she outside?"

"She is under the kitchen table," I replied flatly.

"Under the table? What happened?"

"She started crying, then she crawled under the table, and started sucking her thumb. She isn't mamma anymore."

The weighted silence made me nervous. Finally, my granny came back on the phone.

"Where is your little brother?"

"He is on the couch eating cereal and watching cartoons."

"And tell me, how long has your mamma been under the table?"

I thought for a moment, wanting to be as truthful as possible.

"Granny, I am not sure, but I think three days and three nights, but it could be four. I'm sorry I don't remember the days."

"Can you try to put your mamma on the phone?"

I climbed down from the chair and pulled the cord around to the kitchen table. As I looked down, I held the phone out, but the stranger just cringed and backed away further under the table.

"Granny, I think she is too scared. "

"Your mamma is too scared to talk on the phone?"

"She isn't *mamma* anymore," I repeated.

"Everything is going to be ok. I will be there in the morning, alright?"

"Ok, can you bring more cereal?"

†

By the next morning, my father and grandparents had arrived. It was decided that I should go back to Alaska to stay with them while my mother was in an asylum. My brother was given to some family members, who already had a house full of kids, so one more was not a problem for them. My father returned north to work as a welder on an oil pipeline.

My grandparents had purchased the Sitka Hotel out of bankruptcy and had injected it with new life. As they worked on repairs, it became a well-known and respected landmark in the island community.

I was required to do small tasks during the week—such as emptying the cigarette butts from ashtrays with my little bucket of sand, flipping up the holder and dropping the used sand into a cylinder beneath, then adding fresh sand to the tray on top.

Though I was only six years old, I felt so proud of myself every time I accomplished a task.

I learned how to run the elevator and even got assigned the large responsibility of helping the maids push down dirty linen through the chute, where the little old ladies doing laundry in the basement would look up and thank me.

On Mondays, I would be at the front desk with my grandfather as he balanced his books and tended to guests.

My little life in Alaska seemed so perfect, until… my mother wanted a visit, and I was summoned back home to "pretend" to be a family again.

Every time I would be forced to visit the asylum, I would cringe.

These visits would be temporary, and I would do my best to stay out of the way. Sue, as I began referring to her, would play the part of a loving mother in between moments of passing out, switching personalities, and leaving me alone with the son of her "spiritual family" whom she needed to visit every week.

Sue would claim that she needed to talk about her abused childhood to her "spiritual family." Their teenage son was tasked with "babysitting" me while these emotional talks would take place for hours.

Of course, while Sue was crying about her childhood abuse, her not-quite-seven-year-old daughter was being subjected to her own childhood sexual abuse.

I told Sue I didn't want to spend any more time around Joe, that he put his hands on me, and I didn't want him to.

"He is a bad kid," I confessed to her.

Instead of jumping to my rescue, Sue scolded me for saying anything negative about Joe and his family. She began a long rant about how she *needed* that family, and that all they ever did was help.

I told her *again* that he had put his hands on me where he shouldn't have.

Her reply will stick with me for my entire life.

"He was probably just tickling you. You should be ashamed for thinking anything else. Be nice and don't get him in trouble!"

And there it was, the most detrimental words ever spoken to a daughter. I was shocked, lost, and confused.

To make matters worse, she dropped me off at Joe's family's house for over a week after that. I was entertained and enjoyed riding horses and such, but every activity somehow included an inappropriate act that Joe would come up with.

After months of this, I began helping him hide it. God forbid he got in trouble. My family *needed his family*. He couldn't get caught because it would be all my fault!

At a congregation picnic, I spotted Joe talking to one of my younger girlfriends. I had been about nine years old at this point, and I knew from her body language that she feared him. It was all too familiar. My heart fell.

I suddenly hated that I was not the *only* girl subjected to his influence. In fact, I counted eight other girls from our congregation who endured his advances. Most would not admit it, but their eyes screamed the truth.

Something burned inside of me. I would NOT let my friends be hurt by him. This fueled an incredibly bold move. I marched up to Joe and asked if he could help me. I lied that I wanted to climb a tree but couldn't quite reach the first branch!

Of course, he was eager to put his arms around me in public. He relished the excitement of nearly being caught. As he lifted me up, I turned and looked him dead in the eyes.

"If you ever touch Carry (name changed to protect her) or any other girl again, I will tell the entire world what you do."

Joe froze.

Our eyes locked in a battle of wills, neither one of us wanting to be the first to break away. I felt his piercing stare cut through me like a hot knife through butter until an understanding finally passed between us. He nodded slowly.

The second he let go, a pact had been sealed; I bestowed upon him my silent trust that he would never again hurt any of the other girls in our congregation. (And he never did).

Taking on all that man's cruelty, I bore the full brunt of his wickedness in order to protect my friends from any more anguish. This decision gave me a small amount of peace. I realize now as an adult that being able to prevent the abuse of my friends was the only control I had over my situation or even my life.

This peace made the abuse tolerable.

I became a people pleaser. I would take the blame for anything. Not once did I stand up for myself. *Better I than anyone else* became my motto.

†

At seventeen, every ounce of courage I possessed was unleashed when I told the father of my abuser what had been happening since I was small. He listened quietly, a single tear slipping down his cheek, before asking me to promise not to tell his wife, not wanting her to discover the monster she had raised.

With no power and no way out, I accepted his request without knowing the full implications of keeping this a secret. My bravery was disregarded as though it never existed and swept under the rug. Joe was free to leave town and continue his abuse without consequence.

The elders in the Kingdom Hall chose to keep it all hidden away, they didn't want the world to know that an elder's son had caused 90% of the young girls in the congregation such unimaginable pain. I was told to keep quiet. No one would permit me to alert the police. Again, "I shouldn't get him in trouble."

†

Jumping years ahead, I began following an unhealthy pattern of searching for that same kind of abuser, dating him, marrying him, working for him, and surrounding myself with controlling abusive men, to find a sense of normalcy. I had no idea what a healthy relationship could be.

One evening, shortly after my grandfather had passed away, my entire world began crumbling around me. My rock, the one person that I could trust and rely on, had vanished from this earth.

My abusive husband's voice filled the car as he accused me of unimaginable sins for simply coming home late from work. His words seethed with rage and his fists shook with anger. I glanced at him out of the corner of my eye, barely able to contain my fear and anger.

We pulled into the parking lot of the Kingdom Hall, and he flung himself from the car, striding around the hood with alarming speed. As he reached for the door handle, I hit the lock button without a second thought. At that moment I knew I had two options—allow Douchebag (as I fittingly refer to him in my memoir *Recipe of a Warrior*) to drag me out by my hair like he'd done so many times before or take a stand.

He pounded on my window, screaming at me.

My foot hit the gas and I sped away from the parking lot. I had no path in mind, just drove until I ended up back at home. My suitcase was still there by the door, left there after my return from my grandfather's funeral. I picked it up and placed it in the car before my heart began racing; Douchebag could appear from around the corner any second.

I drove to town with one thought—if I returned I would either be killed by him or end up taking my own life. Something had to change.

The abuse from my husband had grown more intense over the last six years, and a suicide attempt a year ago had done nothing to stop it. It wasn't until I reached rock bottom that I saw what pattern I was living in.

Douchebag was a narcissistic psychopath who could charm anyone. He seemed to find joy in manipulating everyone he met.

He immediately began spreading lies about me to alienate any help I might receive from friends, family, or people from the Kingdom Hall.

Of course, everyone believed his lies because I had been the *perfect wife* who hid the abuse from everyone; it's what I was taught to do from age six! So how could anyone think that Douchebag was an abusive husband? No one ever heard me say anything negative. No one ever saw the bruises, no one knew he would kick me down our stairs and then rush to the bottom to comfort me and play hero. I had done everything to keep him from getting into trouble.

With zero help from my friends and family, I used all my resources to stay hidden from my ex-husband. For seven years he would stalk me, find me, and drag me out of movie theaters or parking lots by my hair, to "have a conversation."

He would repeatedly be arrested for violating the protection order, then released the same day, due to overcrowding, and begin stalking me again.

Keeping myself safe spurred a heightened sense of intuition, and I began to recognize traumas in others around me—abused co-workers, children at my son's school, and more.

This gave me a sense of purpose to become a voice for those who had lost theirs. I began researching women's groups, self-help, and meditation techniques formerly unavailable to me as a Jehovah's Witness.

Eventually, this path led me to Hypnotherapy and Life Coaching.

With Hypnotherapy I found that by addressing my own past traumas with specific techniques, the effects of the trauma were lessened, and my emotional reaction nearly vanished.

This was huge! I could erase the victim inside and replace it with the warrior I was meant to be.

I couldn't erase what happened in my past, nor would I want to. Because everything I have gone through has given me a tool, a sword of peace.

Finding the avenue in which to use these tools like Hypnotherapy, Guided Meditation, and Life Coaching have all given me the opportunity to help others find their voice!

Supporting abused women and children, and giving them strength to wield their own swords, is now my new life's purpose.

Sincerely, Cheriess Maree

Please read the full story located at
"Recipe of a Warrior" by Cheriess Maree.

www.AcceleratedExcellence.com

Daniella Corsetti

DC Selfguidance
Coach

https://www.linkedin.com/in/daniella-corsetti-139747a2
https://www.facebook.com/daniella.corsetti
https://www.instagram.com/dc.selfguidance/

I want to be able to help as many people as I can. Showing you how we go from being in that dark place, or not understanding what is going on, to being remarkable and activating the powerful person that lies dormant within you. To be able to bring out that bright light that we buried down deep inside while growing up. How you can overcome your fears and anxiety is all up to you…and you alone can make that decision to invest in yourself to become that person. I can show you the tools and keep you accountable! You were made to live a great life with endless possibilities! Take that first step and activate your hidden power!

Love yourself and others…be kind and stay strong.

Coach and mentor
Daniella Corsetti

BREAST CANCER WARRIOR
FEARING THE UNKNOWN

By Daniella Corsetti

You've got breast cancer!

These four words are so devastating to a vast variety of women. No one wants to hear these words from their doctors.

The first thought that instantly crosses your mind is "How will I get through this?" I would like to share with you all my diagnosis, journey, and story.

I always considered myself an average person. I work a nine-to-five job, pay my bills, and enjoy socializing with friends and family. Being recently single at the time, I was trying my best to get my life back in order. NEVER did I expect what was about to happen—it would turn my world upside down.

Shortly after my birthday in September 2014, I had to go for my annual mammogram which was routine, or so I thought. Days later, I received a phone call asking me to come back for an ultrasound. They found my breast to be dense and they wanted to take a closer look. I was somewhat nervous as to why this was happening now. I never had to do this before. Once the ultrasound was done, I was told to go see my doctor for the results, who at the time was my gynecologist. She then informed me that I needed to go see a specialist.

Needless to say, a whole slew of emotions came flooding through my mind.

I had not mentioned anything to my family as I didn't want to worry them until I had all the facts; however, I knew this was not normal.

Mom was the first one to comfort me by telling me, "It's probably nothing and everything is going to be OK." Fortunately, she came with me to the specialist.

I remember that day like it was yesterday, sitting in that small examination room. Mom and a good friend, Chadi, were with me when the doctor came in. He said, "Well, it's confirmed. You have breast cancer."

That's when I completely blacked out. My heart fell into the pit of my stomach, and I was crying uncontrollably. My world as I knew it would change forever. Meanwhile, all that time the doctor was explaining what our next steps were going to be. I am so grateful for both Mom and my friend being there with me on that day.

Leaving the hospital, I was feeling as though a ton of bricks just landed on my head. I was uncertain of what the next steps were going to be and so unsure about my future. This was a lot for me to say the least.

As I was leaving the hospital, I called the office. The girls wanted to know what the results were. With a heavy heart, I had to tell my coworker that I had breast cancer. We were both crying on the phone as she was trying to console me. I asked her if she could relay the message to the rest of my coworkers as I could not bring myself to tell everyone.

Surprisingly, I was thinking of how I was going to tell Dad. When we arrived home, he knew I didn't have good news just by the look on his face. I could see in his eyes that he wished he could take this away from me, wishing he would go through this instead. Unfortunately, we all know life doesn't work that way. This is something I had to deal with on my own. I needed some time to myself to process everything.

I remember crying myself to sleep that night and letting it all out. As I was thinking about all this, it dawned on me the reason why this was happening to me. I knew right there and then that I needed to change my mindset. I was determined to attack this head—on, and I was going to win. No one or nothing was going to hold me back. I no longer wanted to be a victim of this disease.

I am blessed to have Chadi, who I consider a part of my family. He suggested I go see Dr. Meterissian who successfully treated his mother with breast cancer.

Dr. Meterissian is the head of the breast cancer center at the MUHC hospital. His mom took me to see him without an appointment, and I thought to myself "Wow this doctor must really care about his patients with breast cancer. I would feel relieved if he took me on as a patient."

The first doctor diagnosed me with one lump that had to be removed through a lumpectomy. Since Dr. Meterissian is a wonderful and thorough doctor, he wanted his own tests done and to get an MRI. He took the time to share with me that this is a precautionary measure and that he doesn't want to have any surprises during surgery.

On the day of the MRI, I was accompanied by my friend Linda. I knew this was routine, or so they said. Yes, I was a little skeptical; however, part of me knew I shouldn't worry. Being claustrophobic, this exam made me very uncomfortable. Getting an MRI is not your typical exam. The machine is super loud, I had earphones on and was listening to music. I did not hear any music at the time, only the tumbling of the machine.

Once the exam was over, I was instructed to stay at the hospital in case they needed something. I waited in the cafeteria. Nothing like refueling the body with a good lunch and a good friend; however, the stress is in no way lessened.

During lunch, a nurse came towards us. She told me that I needed to go upstairs for an ultrasound. I thought, "Now what?"

We made it upstairs and the doctor administering the ultrasound informed me that they now needed to conduct a biopsy. Never having a biopsy done, I really did not know what to expect. I now realize that fear comes from not knowing.

In a way, I'm glad the biopsy happened the way that it did so I didn't have time to worry about the procedures. I remember this pencil-shaped instrument being inserted on the side of my breast to get a tissue sample from that area. With a quick and sharp pinch, the tissue was removed. The doctor did this three times and told me that they would insert what they called markers to show that this area was tested.

I managed to go outside and inform Linda about what was going on so that she could inform my family of the latest developments. Later she told me that she was going through a whole brunt of interrogations from my family members. She lightened the mood by making me laugh, telling me how stressed my sister was and how she expected everyone to stop what they were doing and answer our questions NOW. There was not much that Linda could do as that floor only had women getting their mammograms done. So, there was nobody she could ask; the nurses and doctors were all occupied tending to patients. That's my family. I also realized that our support group goes through its own stresses as well.

One week later, the results were in and I went to see Dr. Meterissian. He informed me that the MRI had determined that there were three lumps and not just one, therefore the lumpectomy had now become a mastectomy. We had scheduled a surgery date for the lumpectomy on December 23rd, 2014, therefore he advised me we could change the date so I could have more time to think.

With this new development, he wanted me to really think about the fact that I was NOT going to have a right breast. I would be the one who had to look in the mirror every day and see my right side completely flat. Dr Meterissian wanted to make sure that I would be mentally ok with that.

He explained to me how the surgery was going to go. First, he would take three to four lymph nodes from underneath my right arm, which would go to pathology to test if the cancer had spread to my lymph nodes. This would determine whether he would have to remove all the lymph nodes along with the whole breast.

I came home that night and cried as I mourned the loss of my breast. Once I had gotten this out of my system, I realized that I no longer wanted to be a VICTIM of this disease, but a VICTOR. That was when my mindset changed and I accepted what was happening to me. Acceptance was the key to changing my mindset. Looking in the mirror, I told myself that I was not going to start the new year with cancer. I wanted this removed and out of my body as soon as possible.

The next morning, I called my doctor and I told him to go ahead with the surgery as planned for December 23rd. I now had a different outlook on what I wanted. I wanted to be cancer-free, healthy, and enjoy life to the fullest.

As the date for the surgery was fast approaching, I was determined not to let that stress me out. I made sure I had a positive mindset going into this surgery. I kept telling myself that the team knew what they were doing, that I was not the first woman to have this surgery, nor would I be the last.

Staying in that positive frame of mind helped me to focus on what needed to be done and what I had to do going forward. Once I accepted that I had cancer and that I was going to lose my right breast…well that's when everything changed for me. I woke up the next day after my surgery, looked in the mirror, and said, "I HAD CANCER…CANCER DID NOT HAVE ME." This was a powerful statement.

As this was the Christmas season, there was no way I was going to put a damper on everyone's festivities. I can't emphasize enough how changing my thought process showed me how strong of a person I really am. I was celebrating Christmas with my family two days after my surgery. Yes, I was a little tired, but I took a nap every once in a while and then I was ready to party.

I was often asked by my family and friends who know me, "Why you?" and my reply was always the same: "Well, why not me?" I'm no more special than any other woman.

Cancer does not discriminate. We can be young, old, rich, poor, male, or female—it doesn't matter if the fact remains that "YOU HAVE CANCER."

Throughout our lives we will always be faced with fear; how we overcome it is the game changer.

Going through life thinking "That's not going to happen to me," "That's not my case," "I take such good care of myself and my family," and then the unthinkable happens and we are told we have cancer. Once you learn to let go of the victim mindset your vision becomes clear, you become the victor.

There is another factor we tend to forget: our family members and support groups. They are also going through this with you, and it is important that they feel like they're helping. They are left behind while we are dealing with everything physically. We lash out at them, we ignore them, we dismiss them without reason, and all they want to do is help. My support system was amazing, and I am blessed that I had the support I did. Yes, I'll admit it, I was nasty, and that is when I realized that it's not their fault. They're all here to help and support me. So, occasionally, please thank them for standing by your side.

When I was going through this, there was not that much support that I could reach out to. Therefore I am so blessed and grateful, to this day, for the support that I had from my family and friends.

Asking for help is not a sign of weakness, but rather a sign of strength. We all need help, all we must do is ask; just reach out. Why is this so hard to do for some of us? The amount of help and support that is out there is truly remarkable.

Today I am happy to report that I am still cancer-free. I don't think I would have been able to overcome some of the challenges had I not searched deep inside and found the strength to change my mindset and stay positive throughout the whole process.

This journey has opened me up to the tremendous possibilities life has to offer. I have since become a life coach and mentor. I keep improving myself every day, little by little, so I can be the best version of myself. I celebrate every victory, no matter how big or small.

I want to be able to help as many people as I can. Showing you how we go from being in that dark place, or not understanding what is going on, to being remarkable and activating the powerful person that lies dormant within us. To be able to bring out that bright light that we buried down deep inside while growing up. How you can overcome your fears and anxiety, it's all up to you....and you alone must make the decision to invest in yourself to become that person. I can show you the tools and keep you accountable! You were made to live a great life with endless possibilities! Take that first step and activate your hidden power!

Love yourself and others…be kind and stay strong.

Coach and mentor,
Daniella Corsetti

I am grateful and thankful to my surgeon Dr. Sarkis Meterissian, his surgical team, and the staff at the MUHC.

I also want to share my heartfelt gratitude to my family and friends and express how much their support has made me the strong woman that I am today.

Deborah Corsetti

DC Self Guidance
Self-Love and Mindset Coach

https://www.linkedin.com/in/deborah-corsetti-aa9655248
https://www.facebook.com/debbie.corsetti.5?mibextid=LQQJ4d
https://instagram.com/deb.corsetti?igshid=OGQ5ZDc2ODk2ZA==

Deborah Corsetti is a Spec Ed Tech and Self-Love and Mindset Coach, author, and mom of two beauties.

In 2018, her life took a significant turn when she lost both her parents to cancer and months later divorced from her 24-year marriage. This pivotal moment forced her to dig deep within her own resilience and inner strength. Determined to provide the best possible examples for her daughters, she embarked on a journey of self-discovery that ultimately changed the trajectory of her life. Deborah's passion for helping others unlock their true potential led her to pursue a career as a COACH. Her coaching has been nothing short of transformative for her clients. Through her compassionate guidance, she has helped countless individuals break free from self-doubt through the appreciation of self-love. Deborah is a beacon of hope and a living example of what is possible.

MENDING BROKEN WINGS: UNLEASHING THE MAGIC IN TRAGIC MOMENTS

By Deborah Corsetti

Who would've known January 11, 2018, marked the beginning of a profound spiritual awakening that changed my life forever?

Until that moment, I had never really placed any trust in my intuition; however, on that fateful day, for some reason an inexplicable feeling washed over me, signaling the beginning of the end of my father's life.

That day, Dad was admitted to the hospital for a recurring problem that he had suffered from due to his previous battle with colon cancer.

My father's journey ended five months later, marked by an exhausting battle for survival. The amount of suffering he underwent was not only a testament to his strength but an ordeal for our entire family. From consecutive emergency back-to-back surgeries to untangling his intestines from bowel obstruction, an accidental rupture and removal of his spleen, numerous blood infections, pneumonia due to food obstruction, and a stroke… his list of ailments seemed endless.

His final battle was with liver cancer. How much can a poor soul endure? As he faced each challenge, he fought with every fiber of his being.

Witnessing his pain was agonizing, leaving me with a profound sense of powerlessness. His ordeal led me to question the purpose of our lives and the unique journey we all embark on.

During his ordeal, I remember communicating with him through a whiteboard, providing comfort and support as he faced the unknown.

As his condition deteriorated, he grew quieter and more pensive, reflecting on his life and how ours would change as well. He understood that when the physiotherapists stopped visiting as they did with daily visits it signaled his journey's end.

Two nights before he departed, we had "the talk." By then, he was in palliative care, and I had spent every possible moment by his side, fully aware that time was running out. He knew this was the end.

In retrospect, it was as though he knew what was going to happen years later. He urged me to toughen up, to become stronger and more resilient. Watching my father endure such trials and tribulations, knowing he hadn't led an easy life, led me to question my existence. At that time, I couldn't provide definitive answers; all I knew was that something felt grossly unfair. By then, I started realizing that we have the power to choose how we want to perceive our experiences.

His passing on my birthday, surrounded by family, was a bittersweet moment. His final smile at my mother left a mark on all our hearts. What a beautiful moment. Their love was like no other.

I remember not being able to cope so well and just wanting to sleep for weeks after his death.

Mourning my father's death was the hardest thing I had to do as he was my rock and anchor. Weeks turned into months, and the tears seemed endless. I had continued my leave of absence from work and found comfort in medication to help me cope.

How was I ever going to overcome this grief?

Well, the universe had plans in store, even though I was unprepared for what lay ahead.

Shortly after, while moving Mom to a condo, my ex-husband and I decided to live in my father's home to carry on our family tradition. During this transition, my mom developed a persistent cough that demanded attention.

Unfortunately, her first appointment was canceled due to an intense snowstorm which paralyzed the whole city of Montreal. We had no choice but to reschedule her appointment. After all the necessary testing, she received a shocking diagnosis of lung cancer, never having smoked a day in her life.

How could this even be possible?

I hadn't fully recovered from my father's passing and now I found myself faced with this new challenge. Nevertheless, I stood by my mother's side and accompanied her to all her medical appointments, both of us filled with fear.

The downtown hospital, where she received treatment initially offered us a closer facility considering the many medical treatments that would leave her feeling weak and vulnerable.

Our medical system presented its own challenges with treatment, decisions, and medication that did not always align with our needs. The future remained uncertain, but of course, we clung to hope and practiced faith.

Chemotherapy was our only option as now the cancer had spread to her liver.

It's astonishing how we place trust and faith in our doctors, hoping for healing, and yet in many situations, become subjects in a medical experiment without our knowledge or consent.

Life is short, we do have options and we possess choices and personal power that we easily give away to others without a second thought.

Sadly, none of the medications showed any improvement in shrinking her tumors. Things were not getting better—they worsened as the cancer had now spread to her brain. Mom was undoubtedly the strongest woman I knew; she fought fearlessly and she was determined to live. She never showed any emotions or signs of fear, although we were all aware of the emotions she must have been suppressing.

Her resilience came from her desire to keep me calm and shield me from my anxieties. So, we followed the doctors' recommendations at the time. We were very grateful for their empathy and compassion; however, we couldn't escape the fear-driven nature of our medical system. The brain radiation treatment was unlike the others. This one required a mask to protect her face, to allow radiation treatment to focus only on targeted areas. It took just three weeks of this treatment before I noticed patches of her hair falling out. I couldn't bear all this suffering and wanted to minimize her pain in any way I could.

After all, isn't that what love is all about—selfishly doing whatever it takes for someone else and empathizing with their condition?

On that day, I suggested we go shave her head and find a wig immediately. Mom agreed as her positivity was a ray of light. Finding the perfect wig was challenging, but when we did tears of relief flowed from both our faces. From that moment on, we no longer put up a facade and openly shared our feelings about how this journey was affecting us both. It wasn't getting easier.

For the first time in my life, I felt the difference between mental health and physical well-being. My mind was not in a good place, and I understood the importance of staying strong for my family, especially my beautiful daughters, as we faced everything head-on.

I needed to get away; I needed a chance to breathe and accept and gather strength for the darkest chapter of my life. My mother was understanding; she recognized that, even though we weren't the ones battling cancer, we were enduring the stress and strain alongside her.

By the time I returned a week later, her condition had deteriorated significantly. She was vomiting frequently as the cancer had now spread to the liver. She could no longer be left alone. My sisters and I, alongside her sisters, devised a weekly schedule to care for her, but she refused.

My mother never wished to be a burden to anyone. She, unlike my father, desired her remaining days to be in palliative care.

February 1, 2020, was the day we entered palliative care, and my intuition spoke to me. I told my sister, "Daddy will come get her on Valentine's Day."

This palliative care facility was so beautiful. It offered a calm view of the lake, allowing us to marvel at the sunrise every single morning. I guess this is where my increased love and appreciation for sunsets and sunrises stems from.

She fought so hard, never shedding a tear in my presence. It was like she had come to terms with what was to come next. And during her final days, she remained mentally sharp, voicing her last wishes regarding food and family gatherings.

During her time in palliative care, I had taken an extended leave from work to be by her side every moment. Those days were horrible as I watched her gradually decline every morning. I woke up to a different, frailer version of her until the day came when she could no longer even sip through a straw. I knew her time had come.

On February 14, my intuition was confirmed. Dad did indeed come to get Mom and left a red cardinal behind as a sign of confirmation. It was at this point that I comprehended that these events were not a mere coincidence and that everything happens for a reason, and every experience holds a purpose.

This marked the beginning of my exploration into spirituality, and the universe started blossoming. I feel blessed that I was able to live there, with Mom in palliative care, as those last moments were so precious. Weeks after we laid Mom to rest, I realized my whole world had crumbled. I lost the two most cherished people in my life, my anchor and my best friend. Life would never be the same again!

Once we buried my mom, my whole world fell apart. I felt lost; how was I to carry on like everything was normal?

The universe wasn't finished just yet. Four months after my mom passed, the universe unexpectedly brought a divorce into my life. My marriage was strong for 24 years, but unfortunately, the previous events caused a lot of separation in the process.

Without diving into too many details, I have my perception of things and he has his. It's not about who is right and who is wrong. It's about love, and how things can change throughout the years. It's important not to have expectations about anyone or anything. It's about not playing the victim and blaming others for where we land throughout life.

These events led me to my spiritual awakening. My appreciation of self-love exceeded my expectations as well. I had never loved myself to the fullest, and life allowed me to take the time to do this. Appreciation is the foundation and miracle cure to living a happy life and one you always believed you were meant to live.

I was at the lowest point of my life and my pillars, my mother and father, were not there to help me. I had to hold myself accountable for the rest of my time—only I could decide if I was going to be happy or not.

How was I going to get myself out of this dark place? I was still mourning Dad, then Mom, and by the time my divorce was finalized, I was completely numb. I avoided my emotions because they were too painful to face.

After receiving counseling from a spiritual mentor, I took a lot of time to deeply reflect on myself and my life decisions. What did I want?

What did I wish my life would look like?

It forced me to connect all the pieces of my puzzle from every experience. This journey opened my eyes. It forced me to re-adjust my mindset and set clear intentions so that if I wanted to change my life, I would need to get out of this dark cloud.

The healed version of me is not grateful Mom and Dad are no longer with me in the physical realm, but I am grateful that I was taught all these beautiful lessons. I am thankful to be able to share my story with you all.

I had lost everything. My zest for life, my purpose, and my identity. I was no longer a daughter in a sense and no longer a wife. I was simply Debbie. I was still a mother, and that alone pushed me to grow and heal—for my girls. I wanted to teach my girls to love themselves and find strength within, to pursue anything they put their minds to.

Today, I have done enough of my inner work to acknowledge that the truth is that we both had our reasons for why this marriage was failing. Things are not the way they are because of someone else but rather because of a collaborative effort.

My definition of love comes down to the good moments in life but also being able to hold space for your partner when life doesn't go the way it's expected to play out. The shock and disappointment that our beautiful family endured is what hurts. The feeling of a broken family. It was evident my ex-husband and I were no longer in alignment.

My life changed drastically in such a short time. I look back on my past not with sadness but instead with gratitude for what I have today. I wouldn't be here today if I was not resilient.

I can remember waking up in the morning wondering why I was still here. The mental exhaustion was extremely demanding. The difference between mental health and physical health was evident to me at this point.

My entire being needed healing and I didn't know where to start. This was not going to be easy, but I turned to a spiritual practice to align myself with my true needs and wants.

To leave you all with a valuable message, I wish to say that many of us live life anticipating the worst-case scenarios based on our knowledge of how things should play out or based on our past experiences. Instead, we can choose to believe an infinite number of other possibilities.

We can see our lives through a lens of love instead of being surrounded by stress and fear.

Throughout my journey, I realized that everything does happen for a reason. Allow yourself to flow through life with everything unfolding in due time. The answer to your questions will always show once the storm ends.

What is the point of all this? Life is all what you choose to let it be. You hold the magic cards in your hands. You create your reality and that is what I've been doing since my lowest moments and urging those around me to do as well. In March of 2022, I graduated as a life and wellness coach. I've been working on my practice and ideology ever since.

My purpose and dream is to help as many beautiful humans as I can. I desire to let my clients feel not only content and alive again, but also to awaken their souls and to live through truth and authenticity. You are allowed to be freed from judgment and pressure in the world. Approach life with confidence and unconditional love for yourself.

Self-love is truly the miracle of happiness.

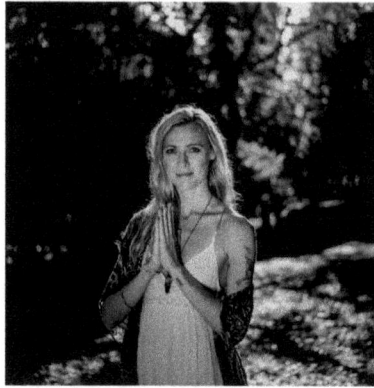

Destiny Wolf

Destiny Wolf Wellness
Transformational Coach

https://www.linkedin.com/in/destiny-wolf
https://www.facebook.com/destinywolfyoga/
https://www.instagram.com/destinywolfyoga/
https://www.destinywolf.com/
https://www.udayaretreats.com/

Destiny Wolf is a Yoga and Mindfulness Meditation Teacher, Sound Healing Practitioner, Breathwork Facilitator, and Ceremonialist based in Sydney, Australia. She offers movement, breath, meditation, and sound practices to help others feel nourished, connected, and empowered on their journeys. Destiny's passion is to help people find what lights them up and then follow that light to shine bright. She is the founder of Udaya Retreats where she hosts international wellness retreats and Alive Tribe Journeys where she creates multisensory wellness, music, and art events to help the community connect and celebrate what it is to be alive and surf the waves of existence.

Destiny grew up in the US in a musical family and began writing songs from her primary years. She spent a lot of her youth singing but lost her voice in her young adulthood due to traumatic events. She found her heart's song again 10 years later after experiencing sound healing and working with crystal singing bowls to open her throat chakra. She is passionate about the power of sound and how these vibrations can help reset the nervous system, promote deep healing, and greater internal balance.

When she's not teaching, you can find her strumming her ukulele, dancing, or enjoying ocean swims in her neighbourhood in Sydney.

Destiny's biggest inspiration comes from the footsteps she's travelled across the planet, and this universal connectedness infuses her offerings as she draws from Native American lineages from her roots in Arizona, Eastern Asian Buddhist teachings, modern scientific Western practices, and South American Shamanism.

You can connect with Destiny and find out more about how to work with her on her website: www.destinywolf.com.

WARRIOR OF LOVE

By Destiny Wolf

"Stop acting so small. You are the universe in ecstatic motion. Set your life on fire. Seek those who fan your flames."—Rumi

The woman who lives her life on fire is unstoppable. With the fuel of passion, she moves through life knowing she belongs. This woman perceives beauty as a way of living, a way of dancing through life with reverence, empathy, and understanding for all living beings. She feels the heartbeat of the earth under her soles, hears the song of the wind, vibrates with the electricity of lightning in her cells, and breathes the rhythms of connection threaded through human existence.

Darkness precedes light; darkness is integral to this woman's essence and evolution. She is a warrior of love, speaking for the voiceless and sharing her story as a beacon of light. Her scars are part of her power; through them, she shines brighter. Self-love made her a lighthouse. She touches hearts, unties blindfolds, and unleashes people to feel their own healing powers. She helps them touch their deepest selves and listen to the whispers of their calling. She dedicates her precious days to helping others commune with their truth, mitigating humanity's suffering.

I, Destiny Faith Wolf, am this woman. Let me share with you the wisdom I have gleaned on my journey; the wisdom which gave me phoenix wings as I rose from the ashes, burning with love. I live my life on fire. So can you.

Soul-Song

There's an innate soul-song within us all, longing to be expressed and heard, to harmonise and flow. Like a young kookaburra chirping melodies in the nest at the morning's first rays, some babies begin cooing, humming, and vibrating to the rhythms of life weeks into their entrance into this mysterious world. That was me. I was humming, awing, and expressing myself from the nest through sound.

Growing up in a large family, music was our ride or die: we sang and played guitar, piano, violin, and trombone. Despite the financial struggle and the turbulence of relocating six times in a decade, music was our magic carpet. Sunday mornings were for singing together, a Wolf pack howling its heart out. In this energy of openness, as a girl, I would process my emotions and share my truth by creating songs, raps, and poems.

Song was my love into my teens until the day I lost my voice. I was 18 years old, unable to express myself. Traumatic events stole my power and silenced my voice. For a decade I stopped singing.

Am I too sensitive?

I felt a lot growing up. I was a highly sensitive, empathetic child. When another person was suffering, I would feel it and want to help fix it. When I was upset, I learned to mask my emotions and cry in the closet so I wouldn't appear weak. I didn't want to be overly emotional and ungrateful. I wanted to do my best in life, and this translated into perfectionism. I graduated Salutatorian in my 8th-grade graduation and was unhappy that I wasn't at the top. This carried on throughout my teens and into university where I graduated Magna Cum Laude, with Honors awards, and felt disappointed. Nothing I did was good enough. I didn't like myself to the point that I called the suicide hotline in junior high as I felt guilty my parents had to deal with me.

A lovely mask concealed toxic, high-performing perfectionism. I used wit and humor to make people like me and feel validated. There are powerful gifts on the other side of our pain points. With time, the mask welded to my face became suffocating. I needed to escape the pressure of seeking external validation.

Numb

Alcohol let me turn off my brain. I felt wild and free. One night the summer before my senior year of high school, I ended up at a college party (in actuality just an apartment full of college boys). They gave my friend and me these sweet red drinks called Jungle Juice. I started to feel foggy. I was lured into a room. The door locked behind me. I was shoved onto the bed. Couldn't move; couldn't speak.

"Leave man, she's mine," one guy muttered.

Mustering all my energy, I begged him to stop, that I had a boyfriend.

"Be quiet and everything will be ok," he warned, undressing. He started assaulting me. Before he could rape me, my friend broke down the door and whisked me out of there. I was violently sick from the drugs that were laced in the jungle juice. I vomited blood.

That was the night I started losing my voice. Stripped of my freedom and power; I needed help. Yet I blamed myself and was sucked into a vortex of shame and unworthiness, becoming alienated from within.

Isolation

Over the next seven years, I survived multiple sexual assaults, in silence, and numbed myself with marijuana and alcohol. My inner world was a dark, lonely place. By 21, I hated myself. I revealed the assaults to the doctor and was diagnosed with depression, anxiety, and insomnia; I was put on Lexapro, Xanax, and Trazadone. The medication got me through college (working 30 hours a week to pay for school fees), but I stopped writing. I'd already stopped singing. Now I stopped expressing myself completely. On the surface, my mask was still welded on, and I excelled at university.

The summer after graduation, a cute colleague offered me a painkiller to help my hangover. Suddenly we were in his convertible, smoking oxycontin off aluminum foil, and I became addicted. After a few months, having blown my money on these pills, I was lying on the couch, numb. A voice spoke to me:

"Destiny, it's time to dig yourself out."

It was destruction or life. I chose life.

Living

When you listen to the call of your heart, the cosmos begin to collaborate with you, opening windows and doors; but it's up to us to pay attention and listen. At 23 I let my heart lead and set off for Wuhan, China to teach. I was ready to create change, although I was scared, lonely, and vulnerable.

One night I went to a club. I was so happy to be out socialising with new friends. We had a VIP table; the owner offered me a drink, my first and only one that night. It was drugged, and I was violently raped in the backroom. There was no singing or humming after this.

Sometimes the deepest darkness, the biggest crack, is where the most powerful light can enter. I didn't think I could survive after this wound. I was so isolated from the shame. I realised that I was the only person who could help myself. I went off the medication cold turkey. I devoured every self-help book I came across and started to teach myself how to meditate. I started to learn how to love myself and nurture my wounds.

Connecting with Love

Amid the darkness, I sat with myself one night, meditating on love. Quietly sitting there, a massive healing began to occur within me. Time stopped, my body vibrated, and tears streamed down. I felt the presence of real love. I met God. I knew I wasn't alone and that someone had been looking out for me throughout the years.

After four years in China and travelling the world, I moved to Sydney, Australia to be with my partner, landing an administrative job at a university. After work, I would dive into my yoga practice. The mat was the mirror where I would start to meet my soul deeper, peeling back the layers and shedding many tears.

One night, after partying with friends, I sat alone on the balcony while *Somewhere Over the Rainbow* came on the shuffle playlist. I cried and felt a pull in my heart to sing again. My soul was calling me home. The next day I stumbled upon a ukulele stall: it was a sign, and I bought one. The vibrations and happy strums of this island instrument brought me back to my roots and my inner child began to express herself once more.

A Life-saving Sting

After completing my first yoga teacher training, my life started shifting dramatically. I survived a near-death experience while scuba diving on a secluded island in Malaysia when a large jellyfish stung me while I was 50 feet underwater. I was not ready to go yet. I wasn't ready to die. The ordeal propelled my healing journey. Clarity descended upon me: nothing is certain in life except the present moment.

Holistic modalities accelerated my return to love including yoga, meditation, breathwork, and sound healing. So dramatic were the changes that I felt the call to share these techniques to help people feel more connected and empowered. I volunteered for Mood Active at a children's hospital, sharing the power of sound with teens suffering from mental illness. It wasn't a question of performance, but of connecting to the deeper rhythm and vibrations of healing, positivity, and human connection.

We are Connected

My journey of sharing sound started by volunteering with A Sound Life, an Australian charity that brings music, meditation, and yoga to people in need. I mustered up the courage to use my beginner ukulele skills and sing regularly at a disability centre for young adults.

During the Covid lockdown, I spontaneously ordered a Happy Drum. Beating it released much fear and tension. Working a 9-5 corporate job, on the computer all day, and isolated from in-person interactions, I felt the lingering darkness from my wounds creeping back in. The vibrations helped me release massive, stuck emotions, stress, and tension, awakening a dormant and powerful force within. I began hosting powerful Sound Healings. I became my own best healer. I dove into Rebirthing Breathwork, transforming years of trauma in my body. Anxiety dissolved. I morphed from a survivor to a warrior of love.

Answering the Call

I quit my job and started a full-time business leading movement, music, meditation, and breath practices to empower people along their journeys. Since I leaped, doors have opened and opportunities flooded my way. Alignment with our heart's purpose is potent. The universe conspires with you to make magic happen. It doesn't come without focus and effort though; it takes dedication. I have worked hard and have learned to take the rejections as redirections. The joy of my work is boundless and immeasurable as I am in my purpose.

My soul song has taken me farther than I could have ever imagined. I am the founder of an International Retreats company that delivers transformational retreats to empower clients to pursue their dreams, and am co-founder of a conscious community, Humans Alive, to help unify people through multi-sensory events with movement, breath, meditation, music, and art. I've had the privilege of speaking and singing at international festivals with thousands of attendees and working with individuals 1:1 to help them rise to overcome their greatest obstacles and limitations, become their own best healers, and live their lives on fire for their purpose. My clients have experienced and testified to feeling more self-love than they've ever felt in their lives, healing from birth traumas, connecting with loved ones who have passed on, getting sober, trusting intuition, healing from chronic pain, and feeling the threads of connection that bind us all together in the tapestry of life.

My message to share with you now is to do the work to meet all parts of yourself. Meet the parts of you that need your love and care, and need to be seen. Meet the parts buried in the darkness that you are afraid to visit. You are strong enough to go there. Once you meet all of yourself, learn to be kind and tend to the parts of you that need your love the most. Love is always more powerful than fear, and the heart's electromagnetic field is stronger than the brain's.

The word for the heart chakra in Sanskrit is Anahata, meaning unstruck. This means you have everything you need within you already to get where you are going. It's just about looking deep inside to access the power of your love, wholeness, and belonging. So, what are you waiting for? The world needs to hear your soul song. Sing!

Live Your Life on Fire

For those of you who have lost your voice or a part of you has gone asleep, this is your sign to wake up. You are strong enough. Here are some of the key steps that enabled me to become who I am today.

Self-love & compassion

Without love for yourself, you won't value yourself enough to even consider that your soul has a unique song and a purpose. Life will always bring new challenges and space to deepen and grow, so self-love is something we must continually commit to. The core of our being is made of love. It is the vibration that threads through us all and never runs dry. The key is softening all the blocks we have towards receiving it and giving it away to allow it to move in us and through us.

Make it real: Place your hand on your heart every morning, first thing, before you even get out of bed. Take five slow, deep breaths, in and out, slowly. Then ask yourself: How am I today? Is there anything I need today? Set one kind, intentional word as an anchor to keep coming back to and help you feel supported.

Explore, recognise & identify your values

When you begin to truly love yourself, you will understand that you are important and you will want to get to know yourself more. Finding out what your most important values are is essential to fulfilling your soul's calling. They might shift and change from time to time slightly but these values are the foundations for your actions.

For example, my top three values currently are:

1. Compassion for all living beings.
2. Growth – always learn and remain open-minded. Stay open to receive new insights and flow with life.
3. Respect and boundaries.

Make it real: Reflect on your values. What is important to you? List your top three values and what they mean to you. Write them down and know your values. Adhere to them.

Regulate your nervous system

Commit to a daily practice that helps you become aware of your body and how you feel to help you find more balance in your life. The body is always present and when we train our awareness to come back to our body, we can experience more of life.

Make it real: Commit to at least one practice that regulates your nervous system and be intentional about how many times a day you want to do it. Whether it's meditation, yoga, running, breathwork, or a quiet walk—connect with yourself.

What is your message?

Imagine you're standing in an auditorium full of people. It's the last day of your life and they are there solely to listen to you. What would you tell them? What words of wisdom and advice for life would you impart to them?

Make it real: Write down your message as if you were giving a speech on your final day of life and imparting your wisdom to your attendees. Keep this somewhere special so you can refer back to it and update it from time to time.

Finding your purpose

What is it that lights you up? What makes you feel alive the most, tugs at your heartstrings, what is your soul song?

Make it real: Create a visual brainstorm with you in the middle and list down all the things in life that you love, are interested in, and that stimulate you. Go wild. List everything. Then choose your top three, explore why they interest you, and list practical ways you could pursue them more.

Elisaveta Saura Kuleshova

Elisaveta SK
Quantum Narcissist Abuse Recovery Mentor

https://www.linkedin.com/in/elisaveta-sk/
https://www.facebook.com/ElisavetaSK1/
https://instagram.com/elisaveta.sk
https://www.elisavetask.com/welcome-phoenix
https://www.elisavetask.com

Elisa is a quantum narcissistic abuse recovery coach, mentor, energy healer, and art & music artist. She guides men and women on their journey of transformation, from deep trauma rooted in CPTSD and narcissistic abuse, as helpless victims, to THRIVING VICTORS in feeling happy, joyful, confident, and loving themselves FULLY again in their multidimensional, cosmic selves.

PHOENIX RISING: MY STORY

By Elisaveta Saura Kuleshova

I wasn't always a victim of emotional or psychological abuse. Not like this. Or at least, that is how my brain allows me to remember.

From early childhood, I remember being the perfect child, the perfect daughter. Life was good. Times were definitely way calmer. I do remember, however, some things that I started to question later. For example, I was never allowed to hang out with other kids that were outside of my parents' friends' children (and if so, they were acting hostile and distrustful of them). Growing up I remember many things my parents did which I thought were normal, so I never questioned them back then.

One of the happiest memories I remember from my childhood was meeting my girl best friend, with whom I shared the same name. I remember sitting alone as I always was in the chairs of a big room, while my mother took part in the organization of the end-of-the-year. Christmas play. I then suddenly noticed a girl my age sitting on the chair to my right. I looked up and saw my mother talking to another woman. I don't know how, but the girl and I started to chit-chat, and I found out we were name twins. We are still friends to this day.

The "downhill sloping" started when I was around 16-17, and I was mid-exam period, stressed as hell. I was sleeping four hours per day, and I remember I had lots of assignments which my mother offered to help me with. I accepted her help, as I always did, but it wasn't until those months that I started to notice how she was playing the victim, telling me "how miserable she is, that she is helping me, but I act so ungrateful." I always ignored those remarks, and it wasn't until those days that I fully started to become aware of how much they hurt (also coming from me, a naturally sensitive person, highly intuitive, and empathetic).

The next morning, barely slept; I went to my high school classes. Next thing I knew, I woke up in the ambulance. And I remember it in a funny way because the first thing I literally thought of when I regained consciousness was "Oh fuck I'm totally missing out on the exam today, mom will be so upset." Looking back now, I realize how my entire life revolved around my mother's expectations, wishes, and goals for me. Because of the confusion, overall stress, and anxiety of meeting my disappointed mother after this experience, I started sobbing right there. The paramedic who assisted me (a very kind young man) talked to me about my situation and offered to talk with my parents about going to therapy sessions. But before that, I was carried to the hospital.

And this is where my nightmare began.

After some tests on my brain, I was not only diagnosed with anxiety but also epilepsy. The latter left me in total shock.

I wasn't the perfect girl my mother wanted me to be. I wasn't the perfect daughter or the perfect student. I wasn't. Because now all my parents saw was a mentally disabled girl.

My phone was taken away whenever my mother wanted. One of the things she used to do was give it to me as a reward, only after I let her do "work" on my face, getting all my pimples out. I hated it, and only complied to talk with the friends I had from high school. I wasn't a very social girl, so I always struggled to make friends. Those who left me hurt me so deeply.

Back to my epilepsy diagnosis, I had to process it for a couple of days, but my parents' treatment wasn't the same anymore. My phone was confiscated at night as well to monitor my sleep because I usually stayed late chatting with people online to practice my English. I didn't realize it then, but I was slowly sinking down, into the deepest depression. Yet, I masked it. I didn't have anybody who understood me, neither did I feel like telling them I was an epileptic. They would see me as "broken" and "imperfect." I was isolating myself more but keeping a smiling mask for my family and friends; that was what was expected from me.

I gradually decided I had to start seeing what I could do too. I didn't subscribe to the idea that I would be stuck with this neurological condition until the day I died. I craved every piece of information to prove my intuition was right. For example, my family's doctor mentioned that because I was only 16, there was a possibility that if I took care of my sleeping schedule, I would recover from this. So, I held onto that hope.

A bit of deeper context here: since I was a child, I was already familiar with the spiritual and metaphysical world. I loved the fae, and from there I got in touch with white magick for the first time. I loved the idea of helping people and providing healing. My fiery mother who was educated in a very masculine environment that often repressed feminine energy (post-Soviet Russia) often didn't share my views about the world. I felt her try to mold me into a respectable, educated student with a good career. I felt this was subconscious programming that was established in women from her lineage to survive in a male-dominated world. In my teenage years, I "accidentally" (I don't believe in coincidences) stumbled upon a post in the magick forum I was in about *starseeds*. The more I kept reading, the more I felt it resonated. I finally felt understood, from a very deep level within myself. I remember it was a day on the weekend when my parents were shopping, and I was home alone. I burst into tears, crying while watching a 25 minute video on YouTube called "Family of Light Wake Up Call."

Something inside me finally clicked. I finally understood who I was, and what my purpose was.

This realization helped me a lot later on with my battle against epilepsy, and everything I held as the "ultimate truth" further down the line. I KNEW physical or mental health conditions can be healed; I just had to find the core root, the reason a person had them.

I mentioned before I struggled with anxiety—I quickly began to realize why.

My mother was rarely happy with me. I remember the nights I had to rewrite entire paragraphs for my school essays because if I messed a word up, I couldn't just erase it, so the entire paper was torn. Math was a real struggle, and my parents had to hire four math teachers before I finally got comfortable with the last one. I struggled with perfectionism and fear of disappointing people. Even with epilepsy, I never wanted to be seen as someone who wasn't useful (smart, quick to complete tasks, reliable). When my mother (or father, because he started doing this too) got upset at me, they used to call me names, insult me, and mock me (e.g. how "useless" and "stupid" I was). This, of course, affected my self-esteem. I also battled with body insecurities – my parents constantly made remarks about it, calling me a "stick," telling me "I had no butt," and "skeleton"… Of course, one complaint and they told me it was just a joke.

Since remembering my soul's purpose, my psychic gifts awakened. I began to have crazy dreams I started to write down: some were past life memories in other planets and dimensions, others were post-apocalyptic scenarios (I think those were common back then with people), and even premonitory ones that always came true. I also began seeing and feeling people from the other side, which was something I had to get used to because my family simply did not want to understand. I took all the energy healing courses, Reiki levels 1 to 4 specifically, to learn to heal myself—body, mind, and soul.

My conclusion as the years passed by was that I did NOT feel safe, AT ALL, and was highly ungrounded. This often happens to people living with dysfunctional families. In a healthy environment, your body functions normally, protects you, and regulates itself when needed. In an abusive household, your body's (and the nervous system's) main goal is SURVIVAL. You're constantly watching what the next threat is going to be (in my case, my emotionally unstable parents), and trying to keep the peace and quiet of the family. That was my self-assumed role for the next few years. After graduation, I started to get tired from all of this as I learned more and more about trauma and mental health. Why pretend I was ok?

I also started to ask some of my friends in high school about my mother's behavior and habits. The control over who should be my friend, the conditional, breadcrumbed love, the silent treatment when she was angry at us (my father and younger brother had to deal with this too), the isolation and attempts to brainwash me into thinking everyone outside the family was an enemy, the verbal abuse, and the times she played the victim to make my father punish me by hitting me… It definitely was NOT normal.

Surfing through the web, I came across the term "narcissist." And even though my mother wasn't "officially" diagnosed by the therapist I went to, (which, by the way, only lasted one month as they decided it was enough) all the traits were describing her. I dug deeper into all the articles, videos, and podcasts I could. Maybe I wasn't the problem as she always claimed I was after fainting that day and getting diagnosed as an epileptic. Maybe someone else was causing it. And I had her in front of me all this time. The reason I couldn't ever feel safe.

So from that moment onward, I started to release and detach from this idea that my mother was right about everything and that all she said was the ultimate truth. It finally hit me. I started to literally absorb all the information and knowledge I could find on the internet about narcissists—the types, their manipulation tactics, how they think and act, their origins. I watched YouTube, read articles online, joined Facebook groups with survivors, and listened to podcasts; every piece of content was worth thousands for me. Speaking of value, I also invested in courses and certifications to boost my healing and recovery. From energy healing like Reiki (master teacher now) to different modalities and approaches to heal and transmute traumatic events like EFT tapping, EMDR, the Rewind technique, conscious association and dissociation, cutting cords, psychic surgery, "the safe place," and even manifestation techniques to speed up the process in the most effortless way possible.

Every day, even if I went through different emotional rollercoasters, I was feeling way better with the knowledge I was gaining. Remember, Knowledge is Key. As for my mother, she saw my change in behavior as a "teenage rebellious phase," even though I was already 18-19 by the time I got all this arsenal of tools and techniques. She didn't leave me alone. The more I wasn't paying attention to her demands, the more furious she got, to the point of scheming and creating whole dramatic scenarios so I would be seen as the "villain" of the family (yes, I was the scapegoat!). So, I would be "punished" for my "bad" behavior, when in reality all I wanted was to ask her why she was behaving the way she was.

Yeah, you totally do NOT ask this to a narcissist; they will end up blaming you for literally everything. I still remember her blaming me every time because I vomited "too much" as a child and she had to take care of me. It is what is expected from a mother, and she didn't like that. Other times when she played the victim because I didn't want to give her my phone—a phone I paid for myself when I was already 18— she would wake my father up from his sleep (he slept early because he had to work early for work too). Of course, my father was furious every time, so it always ended up with physical abuse. I have vivid memories of me hiding either in the wardrobe, or below my desk, so he wouldn't hit me. And the most traumatic thing of all was watching horrified when he did so, and my mother did absolutely nothing to stop him; she was just watching as I received my "punishment" for misbehaving. In time, I learned to protect and defend myself, but I had to be careful not to "overdo" it because they would get even more aggressive. I learned the key was shutting the door to my room and leaning all my weight on it when they both got aggressive.

This of course happened in the last two years of my stay in that household before I left. I never gave up. I could cry, but then I always made sure to stand up again. I noticed the more I was building myself up, planning to leave, building my own coaching business in the mental health industry, and starting to help clients all over the world, the more angry they got. Seems as if they subconsciously knew I could not be controlled anymore.

June 24th was the day I officially left that household with the help of my friends from university.

The day I never looked back. And the start of the No Contact period. Now, I'm watching my business grow as I'm hiring my team at 21 and offering unconditional support and love to everyone in my private group on Facebook, "Becoming PHOENIX Recovery, Healing and Support from Narcissistic Abuse." My 13 week program with the same name offers a transformational journey with all the wisdom, knowledge, and modalities I learned as part of my expertise throughout those years. Years that, honestly, if I didn't live through I wouldn't be living now with my soul life purpose, in full abundance, away from the poverty and family abuse I come from – but which I do not identify with. I know I am not a victim, but a victor.

I couldn't be more grateful to be writing this chapter. And for anyone reading this, survivor or not, know that you're never alone. Your inner child always loves you, so please, stop neglecting them yourself.

Unconditional self-love and acceptance are what we all need nowadays, and it's what my focus is.

If the narcissist is the destroyer of your life force, your vitality, I'll be your hope and love for a brighter future to remind you that YOU ARE THIS TOO.

Heather L. Jefferson

Blessings in The Desert
Blogger

https://www.linkedin.com/in/heather-jefferson-b688b140/
https://www.facebook.com/heather.jefferson.58
https://www.instagram.com/heatherjefferson /
https://www.blessingsinthedesert.com

Heather L. Jefferson was born in Chandler, Arizona but grew up in the Ozark Mountains of Missouri. She returned to Arizona later in life after meeting and marrying while in the Air Force. She has now found home for over 20 years in the beautiful Sonoran Desert of Arizona. Having endured many traumatic and severely painful experiences, she is not a stranger to living a life led by destructive decisions and a self-serving focus. Just existing each day with the temporary highs of worldly happiness, not knowing her purpose. When she was healed by a genuinely loving relationship with her Lord and Savior Jesus Christ, she realized her passion in life was to help others desire a real relationship with God too. Planting seeds of hope and watering the seeds planted by her fellow brothers and sisters in Christ is Heather's most powerful motivation to write now.

THE PIT, THE LIGHT, THE FREEDOM

By Heather L. Jefferson

I could sit and tell you my story of woe. I could expound upon every tedious detail of a daily survival effort that was not consciously sought at such a tender age. I could recount the roller-coaster existence that most would not willingly take even a minute to sit back and reminisce over once the escape from that life was made. But my story would be no more or no less than countless others who have endured such hardship. No… instead, I want to share with you my story of victory. The part where the protagonist rises above the muck and the mire of her trials, climbs out of the pit from her past, and is wiped clean of the residue that was left behind from an early life of aimlessly wandering through a dark and merciless world. I would rather tell of this in hopes that you would gain even the smallest gift of faith to claim your freedom from your own weighted past. I pray you are blessed as well with the gift of leaving behind, no, dying to, the person who was shaped and molded from every abuse, sickness, and unfair tribulation that a broken and fallen world so generously hands out.

Sometimes it's not until later in one's life those heavy trials are given. It doesn't matter when really. These struggles are equally a personal hell each of us must bear. Sometimes it is from birth and on through the first half of their life. For me, it was just that, though I did not know it while I was in it. Honestly, I didn't even ponder it. I assumed it was just normal life. In fact, as a child, I would say I never even considered what another's life consisted of, whether it was easier or better in some way. What is normal after all? So, I continued, stumbling through life day after day just rolling with the punches. I look back now and realize I was no stranger to abuse of all sorts, and not all was due to just one pitifully broken and lost soul. No, the enemy had an army of wickedness that was dispersed through several incredibly sick and depraved souls.

Long after I was far enough away from that corrupt forest to turn back and see each and every demonic tree, so to speak, I used to wonder why it seemed like the enemy had it out for me. It appeared he was always there, never giving me even the slightest minute to rest, whether it was the nightmare I lived during the day or the night terrors that played in my mind at night when I was so desperate for sleep. It felt as if the enemy took sheer pleasure from tormenting me. At the time, I wasn't aware of what was there, but now that my eyes are open, I can clearly see there was an ungodly presence in my life. I learned later that it's not the way I was meant to live. It's not the way any of us are meant to live. At least not by the Creator's design.

It wasn't until I was married, had two children, and was well into my 30s that my heart was touched with the need to know Him. I had heard about God my entire life. I was raised in a small midwestern church, surrounded by mostly family and friends who were like family, but churchgoing for our immediate family was intermittent at best. When we did not grace the door of that quaint little brick building on Walnut Street, we would sit on the floor in front of Dad and listen to stories read to us out of the Children's Bible that sat on the top of our pecan brown Curtis Mathis console most of the time. It's funny how you can read the Bible stories, and hear everything about Jesus, but not know Him at all for most of your life. I knew of God, but He was no more than a celebrity that I heard about all the time. I saw lots of "pictures" of Him and heard from other people who said they knew Him, but being completely honest, I had not the slightest devotion to Him other than trusting that what all of these adults were telling me was indeed the truth, and that some gigantic being was watching every single thing I did so I had better always do the right thing. That worked...for a time, but when things got ugly and I was introduced to the perverse side of life at a very unknowing age of five, well, that made it much more difficult. Oh, I would turn to Him when there was nothing else I could do, and I desperately needed someone, anyone, to save me from the ugly stuff. But then, I would conveniently place God back on the far corner shelf of my mind when things were fine. So, many times, I would forget completely about Him when living in pleasant and enjoyable moments. Why would I have someone on my mind constantly that I did not truly love? Spoiler alert! I discovered later He has always loved me, even when I was so unlovable and forgettable in my own eyes. It's incredible the lies we believe about ourselves sometimes!

In my mid-20s everything finally came to a boiling point. When my baby brother of 20 years suddenly passed away in a drowning accident, it triggered every grotesque, painful, and dark memory I had so diligently packed up, locked in the basement of my mind, and walked away from. You see I had spent the years between 19 and 25 working very hard at not acknowledging anything from my past. In fact, I did my very best to escape the memories and anything connected to them. Often it was with binges of strong alcohol and a shiny façade of happiness and fake confidence. I did not want to deal with my past. I did not want to even remember it. In fact, I didn't want anything to do with the girl who tolerated that life, the one who was a pushover and had no confidence and no guts to stand up for herself. The things she had gone through weren't right, and I was well aware of it. Certain words said to her and actions that were done to her were not kind and should not ever be done to anyone. Don't get me wrong! It's not that I was healthy and at peace. I just chose to be oblivious and didn't understand how messed up I really was, and the decisions I was making at that time were just adding to the weight, digging my pit deeper. My body and mind were starting to show the results of this mangled mashed-up fantasy I had created. I was running off my emotions and that is not something I'd recommend anyone to do. I was soon diagnosed as manic-depressive from everything, had no genuine emotions left and had managed to make a perfectly knotted-up mess of my marriage, as well as every other corner of my life. By this time, the girl I had worked so hard to get away from caught up to me. This loser, who nobody actually cared about, who was unimportant, and who pretty much wasted the air that she breathed, was standing at my front door. She brought with her gifts of panic attacks, sleep issues because of the returning night terrors that were more consistent, and of course a huge helping of self-hatred. So much anger. Anger for the loss of a sibling that I had helped raise and who understood my past. Anger for the memories of physical, sexual, mental, and verbal abuse that, hard as I tried, could not forget. Anger for not being brave enough or smart enough to stop those things, and anger that I could not just be done with it all. The insurmountable pain consumed me. There was not a place on earth I could escape. In all the physical pain I had ever felt, this had no comparison, and it bore deep into my soul. Day in and day out I would wake up with this pain, go throughout my day with this pain, and climb into bed with the pain slowly killing me from the inside. Smothering life out of me. Even my husband, my best friend did not know what to do with me.

I found myself on my knees one night with my face on the floor, the carpet soaked from weeping so deeply. Desperately crying for God to show Himself to me. To relieve me of this relentless pain. Take the memories away Lord! I longed to live again. I was walking through life as a living corpse and just going through the motions of existing.

I was baptized at 16 but never knew God personally. He was waiting for me this whole time to turn to Him and ask for help. I would be lying if I told you this glorious light showed up and the darkness went away that night. He did hear me that night, and I slowly developed a desire to read His word. In all my years of reading those children's Bible stories, I never really had a desire to truly understand them or embrace Him. After all, they were just like the fairy tales I read. Nothing that really connected with me or my life, or so I thought.

It was like a wildfire had been lit inside my soul from that moment. I began waking up each morning before the rest of the house was up, just to take in more scripture. I wanted to soak in it and meditate with it. It was like I was obsessed; I couldn't get enough. I had never been passionate about reading the Bible. It was always like reading stereo instructions for me, but I could feel the healing every time He opened my understanding to a new verse or brought a new truth to light, and I wanted more. Verse by verse He revealed Himself to me. Who He really was. Not the God that I had come to know through years of misguidance and, of course, the enemy's deceptive ways. I received a new and fresh gift of wisdom and healing each morning that I dove into His word. It was incomparable. His mercy and immeasurable grace, and I felt it more passionately than anything I had ever felt before. The sun was brighter than usual, and the birds sang more beautifully than I had ever heard. Many of those moments tears would stream down my cheeks. These were not tears of pain and sorrow anymore. They were tears of joy from sweet revelation! Cold heavy chains of unforgiveness, fear, and deep seeded anger fell away from my heart and released my spirit. I wept so much and so often that my Bible is now marked with smudged tear stained words. Day in and day out I sought God and wanted to know His ways. I was on a mission to know Him personally and to know the truth about who I am in Him. I had found a true friend. A tender loving Father who loves me just as I am, I was enough. Every flawed part of me He loved and accepted, and I never had to be worried again about not being good enough to be truly loved anymore. He showed me what real love looks like. How real love acts. I had someone bigger than my fears fighting for me! The enemy had absolutely no power over me, and never would again! I am protected now from the blackness that tried to consume me.

For the past decade the Lord and I have spent many hours together. I can relate now to the old gospel hymns written about walking and talking with Jesus. I could never do that before. Although I had heard my whole life about Jesus and what He did for us, I never knew Him personally, yet He never left my side. He was always there waiting for me to simply ask Him to show me who He is, and in turn, He showed me who I really am. He set me free with truth. Through life tragedies, the wrongdoings of others, and my own destructive choices, I was not living. I was just existing. In my own deep dark pit, and Jesus was the Light I needed all along to lead me out of that pit to complete freedom. He pulled me up out of it, set me on solid ground, dusted me off, and now has given me wings to fly. I will give it all to Him. Instead of seeking my own healing now, my heart is overflowing with the desire to pour out my blessings onto others. God took this broken person and filled the cracks with His love so that now I can be a vessel to carry His word, His Gospel, and His Light of hope to others.

Please, if you are in a place of darkness, if you are struggling with the demons of your past or right now, I implore you to take a deep breath and just ask Him to show Himself to you. The real Him. The God who is good. The God of multiple chances who never gives up on you. Who treasures every beautifully imperfect fiber of your being. He thoughtfully designed you. You are a unique and precious creation of His. You are fearfully and wonderfully made! (Psalm 139:13-14) You were carefully and lovingly knitted together. I am here to tell you that you do not have to stay in that pit or cold dark prison. You have been lied to and deceived into believing that you are nothing, or that you will not amount to anything. There is hope for freedom from it all when the darkness goes away in the powerful light of God's truth and love. All you have to do is ask. I dare you to!

Jamie Haberman

Hospice Buddy
End of Life Coach

https://www.linkedin.com/in/jamie-haberman-2b8880273/
https://www.facebook.com/HospiceBuddy
https://www.instagram.com/hospicebuddy/
https://hospicebuddy.com/
https://medium.com/@hospicebuddy

Over the past 18 years, Jamie has focused primarily on Hospice, Palliative Care, and Oncology in a variety of settings including inpatient and outpatient oncology, patient's homes, skilled nursing facilities, and inpatient hospice facilities.

Most recently, she has been an on-call, after-hours triage charge nurse. Jamie provides end-of-life education, assistance with symptom management, support, and resources to patients, families, and staff over the phone.

Jamie has always loved taking care of the acutely ill, learning about end-of-life, and providing compassionate, personal, and quality care. She is committed to assisting patients and families to understand, cope with, and manage the changes and challenges that take place at end-of-life to promote a peaceful departure from this life to the next and improved healing for families.

Jamie is also a married, Christian mother of six who enjoys spending time with family, playing games, writing, doing crafts, homeschooling, cooking, and learning new things!

HITTING A BRICK WALL

By Jamie Haberman

Have you ever felt so overwhelmed with life, so absolutely done, that you get to that point where you feel like you've hit a brick wall and you don't even know which way is up anymore? You don't know if you're coming or going or if you even want to participate in this race in the first place.

As I sit here on my lanai, taking in the sun, listening to music, wind chimes, birds, and eventually rain, I am incredibly thankful for so many things. I am thankful for life, for my amazing and supportive husband, our smart and hardworking kids, my career, my business and the course that it's taking, and how it's gaining momentum every single day. I'm thankful for the opportunities to meet and connect with so many awesome, empowering, like-minded people who want to see me succeed and help make my dreams come to fruition.

This is incredible. Far more than I had imagined or had prayed for. Life is amazing and I am really proud of myself. How did I go from overwhelmed, depressed, and daydreaming about ending it all nearly every time I got in my car to where I am now?

Years ago, I was at the lowest point of my life. I was working two full-time nursing jobs; day shift in the hospital's oncology clinic and night shift on weekends, providing continuous care to hospice patients and picking up extra at the inpatient hospice center. Some days I was working thirty-six hours straight between the two jobs and wouldn't even go home. I had four children and was struggling every day to make it work.

On top of the storm I was in, I was also not feeling well. I was having migraines for weeks, pain in one side of my face, heart palpitations, anxiety, and severe fatigue. All I wanted to do was take a nap and never wake up. I was sick of hurting physically and I was sick of hurting emotionally.

My entire life I have been constantly having weird complaints. Labeled as a hypochondriac and a complainer, no one believed me. I had complaints about my heart, hips, back, neck, gut, headaches, mystery rashes, never-ending menstrual cycles, and more. My parents had been telling the doctors about weird symptoms since I was a baby, but I was often dismissed. I was "fine."

Once in a while, I would find the courage to stand up for myself and tell the doctor that I thought he was wrong, and I would get another opinion. Those second opinions often found the cause of my complaints and through their care, I usually ended up having a surgical procedure. Finding a doctor who listens is like finding a needle in a haystack.

Although my diagnosis list kept growing over the years, most of my primary doctors, specialists, psychiatrists, and emergency rooms all said the same thing: "You've got a lot of diagnoses for someone your age, but I don't see anything wrong. Here's a pill. You're depressed. Here's a pill. You have bipolar disorder. Here's a pill. It's probably your thyroid even though your labs are fine." I was on 13 different "pills" and felt like none of them were helping one bit.

To add to my stress, my grandfather was dying, I was in major debt, battling custody issues, and was being mentally and physically controlled by my boyfriend who was a narcissistic drug addict who made my life unbearable by stealing every dollar, every ounce of freedom, and every ounce of self-worth that I had left. I cried myself to sleep most nights.

My stress was incredible. I was nothing. No one was going to want a woman with four kids who works constantly. No one would deal with my attitude or complaints. I was crazy. At least, that's what I was told, and I believed it. If I didn't do what I was told, I was guilt-tripped or threatened to have someone "anonymously" report me to my work for stealing drugs or to take my youngest two children away and I would never find them.

I was severely and utterly broken. Lost. Helpless. Drowning in my own self-pity and smoothing it over with alcohol. Something had to give. I couldn't do it much longer.

I didn't grow up in a household where religion or faith was talked about. It was kind of taboo. Those in my family that did talk about it seemed to be ridiculed. I didn't know what to believe. Was there more to this life or are we simply existing without a purpose? I prayed for answers. I prayed for change, but did God even hear me? It sure didn't feel like it. Maybe there was no God.

I had spent most of my life searching for answers. Is there an afterlife? Is there a God? Which religion is "right?" Is there Heaven? I had a deep need to know. I took classes in college on death and dying and I've always been incredibly intrigued with the paranormal and accurate psychic mediums.

When I started in healthcare, I began to witness death firsthand and continued my career in hospice and oncology, growing my desire even more. I went to a few church services but had a hard time feeling the connection. I couldn't help but feel if there was a God, why did my life suck so bad?

I often fantasized about driving my truck into a brick wall median on the road. Quick and painless, hopefully. With my luck, I'd probably survive and be crippled for the rest of my life. I didn't want to be unsuccessful and I didn't want anyone to have to find me, mangled and bloody in a car. That image would probably haunt them for the rest of their lives. Plus, if I was gone, I wouldn't be able to protect my children. Where would I even go when I was dead? So I never did it.

When my grandpa really started declining and nearing the end of life, I started to help care for him in my "spare time" at my aunt's house until he died. When he died, I felt like I did too. I was so done.

Before he passed, I had some conversations with him that really opened my eyes. He told me to "throw that guy out the window" when he was talking to me about my terrible boyfriend. He uplifted me and I knew he was proud of me. I cherish those moments we had.

After my grandfather died, I remembered what he said. I found strength in that memory and at the first opportunity once my ex got arrested, which was really only a matter of time, I immediately went and got a restraining order. At my grandfather's funeral, I told my dad, "I am going to be single for the rest of my life. I'm not going through this again."

Again, I prayed for God to change my life, but was he even listening? Little did I know, he hadn't forsaken me. He was listening. He was working on the back end to sort this out, but I needed to lean into Him to make it happen.

I met my current husband within a few weeks after grandpa's funeral and that conversation with my dad. I am positive that this relationship was "a set up" by God, for him to lift me out of my darkness, support me, protect me, and show me the love that I so desperately needed. We had so much in common. We knew the same people, went to the same school, and crossed paths a million times, but didn't connect until the time was perfect.

A few months into our relationship, life was definitely getting better, but I still felt that life would just not let me breathe. Albeit less frequently, I was still debating if life was worth the work until one day when I accidentally lost control of my new boyfriend's truck while going 70 mph on the freeway. I really did smash into a concrete median, head-on, just as I had daydreamed about so many times.

It was not on purpose, but it proved to be a point from God. I was on my way home from work and it was around 3am. My patient had died so my shift was ending early. I saw something black in the rain-sprinkled road and mistook it for a ripped semi-truck tire. I swerved to avoid the object and before I knew it, I was headed straight towards the concrete median.

Our wedding was coming up and my thought right before the impact was a sadness that I would not be there for it. At the same time, I wasn't scared. I was at peace. I held on, braced for impact, and squeezed my eyes shut. I blacked out as the accident was happening. It happened so fast. But when I opened my eyes, I had landed on the other side of the freeway, facing head-on traffic from the innermost shoulder lane. Thankfully, there was minimal traffic.

My boyfriend's new truck he had just bought was completely totaled. I hit that wall so hard that the truck flew up in the air, flipped upside down, and scraped and slid the top of the truck against the median. When I landed, all of the back windows blew out and all of the tires bent outward and snapped nearly completely off. The front end was smashed in and the bumper was gone. The airbag did not deploy. But, by the grace of God, I was alive.

I did have my seatbelt on. When I opened my eyes, I didn't know what direction I was facing. The road didn't even look familiar. A box truck had pulled over onto the other shoulder of the freeway and called 911.

My phone happened to be conveniently in my lap and I also called 911. My laptop, which was previously on the passenger seat, had hit my right shoulder as it flew past me and landed in the back seat. A sore shoulder was the only injury I sustained. After calling 911, I called my boyfriend and told him what happened. I felt awful that I ruined his truck. Two police officers had to pull hard on the door to get me out, made sure I was ok, and gave me a ride to the police department where my love raced to pick me up.

After this, I started actually praying long and hard about what I wanted with my life. I put my faith in God and knew that I should have died that day. I had prayed for him to change my life and holy cow did he deliver!

This experience made me face the brick wall of my dark fantasy and fall into oncoming freeway traffic, but our gracious God kept me in the emergency lane to keep me safe. When life gets hard, sometimes it takes a true wake-up call to realize you ARE worth it. You still have breath in your lungs and God is not done with you yet! No matter how hard it gets, He will never abandon you.

My faith has grown exponentially as life continued from this point. I put my faith in God that everything will work out one way or another, and there is a reason I am still here, living, breathing, and writing this chapter of this amazing uplifting book.

My faith in God has changed the trajectory of my life. I met someone who supports me and loves me and my children. I found a great job that allows me to work from home, doing what I love. I was able to pull myself out of financial hardship and finally got to the root cause of my medical problems. I was diagnosed with a genetic connective tissue disorder called Ehlers-Danlos Syndrome.

I've asked God to show me my purpose and he answered, opening doors and clearing paths for this amazing journey I am on. In February, I opened my end-of-life coaching business, Hospice Buddy. I help others through one of the most difficult times in their lives and help to provide peace and comfort during the transition from this human existence through death and into eternity with our creator.

I took life's challenges head-on and realized that each hardship was a learning experience to grow my soul and lead me to my greater purpose. I learned to let go of negativity and things I couldn't control and give it to God. I focused on improving my mindset and circumstances, setting and reaching my goals, finding happiness within myself, and most importantly how to be thankful for each and every day.

These experiences, and the path my life has taken since, showed me that God does hear us. Prayers do get answers and God will bring people and circumstances into your life for a much greater purpose. Nothing is a coincidence and there is a purpose for everything, even when we don't understand it. I am thankful for my family, my friends, my life, and my journey. God has strengthened me into the unstoppable woman I am today and I can't wait to see what tomorrow brings!

If you are caring for someone who has been diagnosed with a life-limiting disease or is nearing the end of their life, I would love to be of service and help you through it. I firmly believe that God has put me on this journey of end-of-life care to help others in the best way I know how. He cleared the path along the way and I am now a certified hospice nurse with 16 years of experience. You can reach me at www.HospiceBuddy.com where you will also find a host of resources, educational blogs, and an online store aimed at making caregiving easier.

We are hard pressed on every side, but not crushed; perplexed, but not in despair; persecuted, but not abandoned; struck down, but not destroyed. We always carry around in our body the death of Jesus, so that the life of Jesus may also be revealed in our body. For we who are alive are always being given over to death for Jesus' sake, so that his life may also be revealed in our mortal body. So then, death is at work in us, but life is at work in you. So do not fear, for I am with you; do not be dismayed, for I am your God. I will strengthen you and help you; I will uphold you with my righteous right hand.

2 Corinthians 4:8–12, Isaiah 41:10.

Jennifer Kirkner

Plexus
Brand ambassador

https://www.facebook.com/people/Jennifer-Kirkner/100008050218831/
https://www.instagram.com/kirknerjennifer/
https://mysite.plexusworldwide.com/jenniferkirknerplexus

Jennifer Kirkner was born, raised, and still resides in the Reading, PA area. She is a sister to James, Liz, and Deb Richard. She has been married for five years to Lenny Kirkner IV. She has two daughters Chloe Ohlinger, 22, and Iris Kirkner, 4.

She currently is a stay at home mom, works as a child care provider, and has a social marketing position as an independent Plexus Brand Ambassador. She attends Cocalico Community Church in Reinholds, PA.

In her spare time, she likes to do fun things with her family, attends church functions, volunteers in children's ministries, connects with friends, reads, listens to worship music, and enjoys spending time outside in nature, swimming, attending concerts and live sporting events, and traveling to any beach or warm weather for family vacations.

THE NEW PATH LED BY FAITH

By Jennifer Kirkner

I'm certainly no stranger to struggle in my life. As a Christ-follower for 20 years now, I wanted to share my story of faith and thankfulness during my hard times. These include abandonment from my mother, grieving the loss of my father, teen pregnancy, abuse from a 10-year marriage, divorce, starting again, miscarriage, career disappointment over and over, and a no-cure illness. I share how I make my way through these hard times. I find my faith to be the anchor when everything is shaking, the solid foundation to build on, and the hope in my heart to keep going. I find myself reflecting in thankfulness to God during each of these times. I knew things would turn for the better, but it came with a long path of hurt and healing to get to the new path led by faith.

I endured a 20-year career in the food service management industry. It has been the most rewarding and defeating time I have been through. I take that seriously and I know it would be hard. I'm thankful at a young age I was able to see my dad as a great example of a good work ethic. I went right into the workforce early on.

The start of my career in food service started at the age of 14. I was ambitious to lead, and within six months I was promoted to a training position. This position created a drive in me to lead others. The next step in food service was with another company. I started in entry-level management at the age of 19. At this age, I also had a one-year-old child and was married for a year.

Starting my life as a wife and mother at a young age had so many obstacles. I knew I had to be career-focused to financially support but this was the most emotional time for me. I was not equipped to carry all the burden and it resulted in major depression for most of my life.

The feeling of being overwhelmed most of the time led me to seek God daily. I needed stability, trust, and coping abilities to get through. I am thankful for God's leading, reassurance, and comfort in low times.

The effort I put into work is one way I serve God. I wanted to be a good example for my family. The ability to support financially was rewarding for me. It made me feel good to do that. Unfortunately, it was also a way to distract me from my personal problems. I received promotions with my current company but it got more demanding the higher the position. The ability to receive a promotion always comes with a lot of hurdles to jump. I felt like I made the cut, accepting challenges and finding opportunities for the business. The pressure was high, which resulted in anxiety issues. I am thankful that at this time in my life I embraced therapy. Talking to someone has always been a good outlet for me. I never felt any shame seeing a therapist to talk in private about my issues. It is a way to get my feelings out to another person or seek advice. Prioritizing my mental health was necessary to keep moving forward in my career and for my personal growth. I currently have a therapist that I have been seeing for years, and I am very thankful to God for her kind spirit, for being a great listener, and overall professionalism that gives me tools to overcome many challenges.

Therapy was what I needed to aid me through the tough times I already endured and for what was to come. My lowest moment was my dad's passing. My dad passed away when I was 20 years old. He died of cancer within three months of the diagnosis. He was the only parent I had due to my parents divorcing when I was two years old. My mother had issues of illness and addiction, resulting in her not being in my life. My dad was the role model of a Christian household, honoring God daily and serving in the church. The year of his passing was the same year of my salvation through Christ. I needed saving; life was too hard at that point. It was bittersweet, losing a father and gaining the Holy

Father. This was the time I was so glad to have a personal savior to help me heal from his loss.

The year of the loss of my dad was the same as when I was first abused by my husband. It was when hard got even harder. It was a year I had to start to dig deep in my faith to find my way from dark to light.

It was a situation of staying with him for my child. God clearly closed the door on one final occasion of abuse after 10 years of marriage. I left with the clothes on my back fleeing for safety, filing for immediate PFA and custody, and staying with a coworker with a spare room. I prayed so hard for years about staying or leaving. During this time I was most thankful to God for making the answer clear in my mind and heart to finally leave and for putting a coworker turned caring friend in my path to help me and my daughter.

The same week I left, I received a promotion to the top lead of the store. I was able to benefit from the pay increase. I was thankful to serve in the church during this time too, gaining bonds of emotional and financial support from my peers. I was able to attend small group Bible studies frequently to learn more about faith. I started healing over time, gaining a better sense of self-worth and hope for my future.

Getting to the top, leader position in a store was my goal for myself to support myself and my daughter. I personally drove my development to learn about all aspects of the job, but there were a lot of unknown issues ahead of me. I had the same in-store leader and now an area leader who knew my skills. The situation seemed like it couldn't be any better.

At first, I felt confident being in the same store that I was currently working in and getting the promotion. The team I had were people I already worked with, and knowing their skills was an advantage. I was able to achieve good results overall so I wanted to go to the next step, of course. I wanted to be an area leader in a training store. The expectation was to be nearly perfect in all areas of the business. The goal was within my grasp but it ended in failure. I missed my score by two points. On the next try, I would for sure be redeemed, I thought. It resulted in failing again due to a bench of leaders being indecisive about me personally as a leader. This was a time when I felt like they didn't like me. I took it really personally. I ended up leaving the company after 10 years of employment. This was a huge leap of faith since this was the only support for my daughter and I. I was trusting God for my situation to improve. I am very thankful for my faith at this time as I was hoping for great change in my future and felt that this was the time to move on.

I applied at one place of employment that I had an interest in. Being the right brand for me, I accepted the position and was hired at a comparable wage. It was a financially adjacent move but one rank down. During the interview process, I did speak of not wanting to be the top lead of the store right away. I wanted to go for a promotion, but I wanted to wait until I knew it was the right fit for me. I have the tendency to start strong but wanted to approach this new opportunity differently. I thank God for patience at this time; it was a good decision. It most likely kept me there longer than I probably would have been.

There were many issues with this business right from the start. This was mostly in regard to lots of movement from store to store. There were times I worked at a store for a few days, weeks, months, or years. The workload demand was unrealistic to the amount of staff given on a regular basis. I was determined to succeed and push myself to learn a lot of information on a regular basis to eventually get to a comfort level in advancement with the company.

Shortly after starting with this new opportunity, I met my future husband. It was hard for me to get to the point of pursuing marriage again. I am thankful to God. He led me through the relationship with a new heart. I was healed from my past, learned forgiveness, and was able to openly share and keep pursuing my faith. We started a family shortly into our marriage, but sadly our first baby resulted in a miscarriage. I was taken aback during this time. Thankfully God gave me hope, healing, and strength to try again. About four months later we conceived. My husband stayed home with our little one so I could pursue my goal of promotion.

After she was born in 2019, I was motivated more than ever to get to the next level. The business evolved so much over the years but even through COVID in 2020, it didn't get me where I needed to be. The quality of work and staffing issues were a huge problem for all store leaders in this company to overcome. I had an attitude of resilience during this time to step into what would make me stand out for promotion. I had confidence and hope that my opportunity was within grasp.

My chance in 2021 to be promoted was halted by an illness that brought me to a tough road ahead. The year of the possible promotion was the same as the illness that would change my future career. The illness is called fibromyalgia. It caused me to have terrible body pain resulting in frequent panic attacks. Stress and the physicality of the position were causing pain. I was mentally, emotionally, and physically distraught during this time. I ended up taking a leave of absence due to anxiety because it went from bad to worse really quickly. Risking my health and well-being was not worth it at this point. I am very thankful to have had my faith during this time to help me focus on what really mattered. I had to choose my health over my career. I had to take time to adjust my life to my illness and I was able to stay home with our daughter.

I was already going through the pain management process and was very disappointed in my care. I was given medicine for muscle spasms and did physical therapy and surgical injections in various areas, but my body was having all-over pain and I was hesitant to take pain meds long-term. I wanted to take an approach of gut health supplements to help relieve my symptoms, going an all-natural route. Shortly after taking the products, they helped me. I am thankful that I was able to choose this path because it had such an immediate relief of my symptoms of fibromyalgia. This is an illness that has no cure, so to find any relief was life-changing.

I wanted to share this with others, so I pursued social marketing as a brand ambassador for my beloved gut health products. After a few months of networking, I was approached with an opportunity to write a chapter in a book called Mom Magic. It was an experience of a community of women supporting each other in their networks. It was more than writing a chapter—there were people who had experience to share and other platforms to make income. The new path was set ahead of me. I am thankful for this time when everything seemed like it just fell into place. Success right from the start! I felt like God led the way.

This first experience led to more in the near future. Within months, I had three book projects due to release. This was great for me to be able to share my experiences as a mother and a leader, balancing career and family, grieving loss, and illness being led by faith. The expanding opportunity was to help market the book and to recruit others to write a chapter of their own. This was an exciting time to start a new career endeavor and to build my skills. I was thankful to God at this time for not letting me lose hope, that I have a purpose, and am reassured again that He is good.

I know that my story isn't over yet but I definitely have been led from darkness to light. I hope to take these hard times and issues that I experienced and in turn, help others with God's help. I still struggle, I still ask God why things have to be so difficult. As promised in the Bible, God will not leave us or forsake us. I'm thankful despite going through these hard times that I didn't reject God for the hard life I was given, nor do I see it as punishment for sins. I made it through the toughest times and changed for the better as a result. Looking back from where I am now, I understand. I have been shaped by God into the person I am supposed to be.

Jourdi Bleu

Jourdi Bleu Coaching
Women's Empowerment Coach

https://www.linkedin.com/in/jourdi-bleu-0bb2a738/
https://www.facebook.com/jourdi.bleu
https://www.instagram.com/jourdi_bleu/?hl=en
www.jourdibleu.com

Jourdi Bleu is a Yoga Teacher, Women's Empowerment Coach, and International Speaker. Through her vibrant playfulness, she guides individuals to reconnect with their authentic selves. Jourdi's greatest passion lies in empowering women to gain confidence, clarity, and Fuck Yes Energy. As a warrior goddess who has risen from the darkness of addiction, she now illuminates the path for others to discover their own sparkle. Jourdi's infectious positivity is a driving force, underpinned by her belief that cultivating gratitude and joy leads to a truly fulfilling life. Having split her upbringing between Colorado and Florida, USA, she now calls Sydney, Australia home. A true wanderlust at heart, she travels the globe to share her message of empowerment and hope. When she's not teaching people how to downward dog or speaking on stage, you'll find her diving into ocean waves, dancing to groovy tunes, or discovering new corners of the world.

I LOVE YOU, I AM LISTENING

By Jourdi Bleu

Yoga Teacher, Women's Empowerment Coach & International Speaker

Tears streamed down my face as I was driving around the beautiful Australian coastline to work. I was hungover AGAIN. This time, I was coming down off of a couple-week bender, and it hurt. The shame, guilt, and embarrassment about the way I had been conducting myself was making my skin crawl. How was I still doing this to myself? I knew drinking alcohol was causing all the problems in my life, but I still continued to pour the poison down my throat. My head was pounding as I slowly drove along, trying to prolong the commute to work because I was supposed to teach a yoga class in this state. What kind of yoga teacher shows up to share a sacred practice feeling spiritually depleted and dead inside? Going to preach to others about loving yourself and your body, and then doing the complete opposite in my private life. The inauthenticity was eating me alive.

I had been here before. I had recognized about four years prior to this that alcohol wasn't playing a good role in my life. But I kept trying to convince myself that I could be a "normal drinker," that everyone had party nights sometimes, and that I deserved to let loose. But this time was different. I suppose you could say I was finally sick and tired of being sick and tired. I was on the phone with my mom sobbing, explaining how scared I was to keep drinking as if I had no control over it. I could see into my future at that moment, and the life I envisioned with drinking was one that disgusted and terrified me.

I hung up the phone as I pulled up to the studio. I looked in the mirror to give myself a pep talk, which was really hard that morning. I despised the woman staring back at me. Her eyes were swollen and her skin was red. She was sad and ashamed because she knew she kept self-sabotaging and pretending she didn't know how to stop it. It was too much to look into her eyes, so I closed them to break the contact and started to take some deep breaths.

All of a sudden, I felt the warm embrace of my higher Self – the One Big Energy that connects us all. A thought dropped in that I never had before; I was in fact in control. I did have a CHOICE. I didn't have to be a slave to my addiction anymore. I opened my eyes again; it was a little more bearable to look at her now. I gazed into her eyes with a bit more self-compassion. A voice so clearly came into my head: "Put the drink down and watch all your dreams come true. It's the only thing holding you back."

This was a constant theme for me – living a double life. Pretending everything was wonderful on the outside but slowly dying inside. This is my memoir of addiction, tragedy, luxury, loss, and ultimately one of triumph and coming home to myself. I have learned how to tune in and listen to the Big Jourdi – the authentic one who lives from her heart and gives herself the love that she deserves. I now know without a doubt that the void I was trying to fill with various things throughout my life can only be fulfilled from within; nothing external will satisfy that space. This is the story of how the fairy with broken wings blossomed into the goddess who soars.

I grew up in an extremely loving home in the snowy mountains of Colorado. I was fortunate enough to have the best family a girl could ask for, and I have only happy memories from my childhood. But things took a bit of a turn when we moved to an island in Florida when I was 12 years old. As if the turmoil of puberty weren't enough, transferring schools is a preteen's worst nightmare. I went from being one of the cool, popular girls to being the strange girl from Colorado who dressed weirdly. This is when the core belief of "I don't belong" became deeply ingrained into my subconscious. This single belief ran my life up until very recently. It was the first time I felt that gaping hole inside of me begin to open up.

Like a lot of teenagers in Florida, I started drinking at quite a young age. The first time I got drunk I was 12 years old, and the first time I blacked out I was 14. I remember looking around my room at the absolute mess me and my girlfriends had made, thinking it was actually pretty cool that I had no recollection of how it all happened. From that moment, alcohol became my best friend. My ally that I could lean on to escape the empty feeling of not knowing where I belonged in the world, and the thing that temporarily filled that internal void.

When I was 15, I endured a traumatic head injury in a car accident, leaving the frontal cortex of my brain most affected—the part that's involved in our decision-making and rational thinking. It was a miracle that I was alive. My survival and the fact that I walked away from it physically unscathed was a shock to the doctors. As the weeks went by, it became apparent that the damage was done on an emotional level. The years to follow were extremely dark ones. I slid into a life of rebellion and addiction. The next few years were littered with arrests, car crashes, heavy drug use, overdoses, promiscuity, expulsions from school, a rehab stint, sexual assaults, and many friends' deaths. I ended up addicted to heroin, hanging out in crack houses, and found my boyfriend's dead body after he overdosed. The recklessness scale was off the charts—I was never consciously suicidal, but a therapist once told me the way I was behaving was a reflection of someone not wanting to be here anymore.

In one of her countless efforts to save me, my mom introduced me to yoga. It didn't quite stick yet, but the seed was planted. Here is where my double life began. On one hand, I graduated from high school and university with honors and was even a teaching assistant for Dr. Peter Adler, a respected Sociology Professor at the University of Denver. On the other hand, I would be having lunchtime wine or snorting cocaine in between classes. I would get home at 5am from a night out partying and then be up at 8am to take my physics test—which I always got an

"A" on. I was perceived as the fun, wild "party girl" in those years, the one who was always down to go out dancing and could keep up with the boys on the beer pong table and bong rips. I was very good at pretending that everything was okay, and I'm pretty sure everyone around me thought I was genuinely happy. I now look back on those times and realize I was numbing the trauma of a life riddled with addiction, an overwhelming sense of not belonging, and nonexistent self-worth.

After graduating from DU with my Bachelor's in Criminology (ironic because I was the one committing crimes most weekends), I ended up in a relationship with a wealthy, Australian businessman. It was a dream come true—being whisked away from a life in Denver that wasn't very healthy for me and plopped down into a mansion in Sydney, living a life of luxury. I thought this was going to be my happily ever after; surely a life of love and fancy things would fill that void inside of me, right?

Wrong. It turns out that not having to work and having heaps of spare time and money in your early twenties wasn't all it was cracked up to be. As the years went on with me not having a purpose, I became more lost. I would host fancy dinner parties, go on 5-star holidays and become a "lady of leisure," but not having a purpose of my own only deepened the addiction that alcohol had over me.

My double life continued: on the outside everything looked absolutely amazing. Everyone kept telling me how lucky I was, and according to Instagram, I was living the absolute "Dream Life." But what Instagram didn't show was my mental breakdowns and my mid-morning cries in the park as I walked my dog and sipped vodka disguised in my water bottle. I knew I was destined for something bigger and more meaningful, but my power felt so incredibly out of reach. The rockstar lifestyle that society portrays as status and prestige left me feeling quite the opposite.

Don't get me wrong, there were some really awesome times in those years. I was very grateful for everything that my ex-partner did for me and the times that we shared. But as I rubbed shoulders with lots of the successful people in the Sydney social scene, I began to see that a lot of them weren't truly happy either. If fancy cars, designer clothing, luxury homes, dream holidays, and exotic dining experiences weren't filling up everyone's cup, then what could? Society teaches us that if we "make it" in life and have enough money to buy nice things, happiness will somehow just appear. I was living proof that this wasn't the case. I got really curious about finding genuine joy and began to dig a bit deeper.

I revisited my yoga practice and sought out meditation and personal development work in hopes of finding some answers there. I began to notice subtle shifts happening on a much more profound level. I wanted to know why I felt so much lighter and more blissful after a yoga class, so I enrolled in my 200 Hour Yoga Teacher Training. I learned of yoga's rich history and the whole Eastern philosophy that comes along with it. I began to connect to my higher self, the Big Jourdi – that universal Self that connects us all.

That void inside of me slowly started to feel a little less empty. I wanted to keep learning and stay on the path of what made me genuinely feel good. I began to work with healers, shamans, breathwork, and meditation teachers and regularly attended health retreats. The relationship that I was in broke down, and pretty abruptly all the luxuries that I had at my fingertips for years were no longer accessible. I would be lying if I said that my ego didn't have a hard time with that at first. I had a very skewed reality of what the value of a dollar was after all those years of not having to worry about money or where it came from. This might make me sound like a ridiculously spoiled princess, and it's because I was. But that was my reality for a while, and I know now that it was no coincidence that I had that experience. Everything in our lives happens FOR us, to help us get closer to our true Self, to assist us in growing and evolving. I had that experience of luxury and love to show me firsthand that money and relationships are not what buys happiness. Happiness is an inside job, something you need to seek within. I had this deep knowing that I had something profound to offer the world, and I became thirsty to find out what exactly that was.

My drinking was still an issue, and the yoga, meditation, and breathwork were good on a spiritual level, but I needed to heal the traumas of my past. All the chaos after my accident just got swept under the rug, buried deep into my subconscious to run my life in ways I wasn't even aware of. I sought out addiction counseling, hypnotherapy, 12 Step Programs, and a myriad of different coaches. I slowly started to unravel the hurt, grief, pain, shame, guilt, and anger that lived inside of me and drove my addictions. I traveled around the world to places like India and Nepal, but this time not in 5-star resorts and helicopters, instead in true backpacker style. The fairy was mending her wings, and it was such a beautiful time in my life.

In 2020 when the pandemic hit, I took it as a time to go inward and discover my path, or my dharma, in this lifetime. It felt very rewarding to pay my own bills with the hard-earned money that I made. I was managing yoga studios, dove into teaching yoga, and started my sobriety journey.

Since then, I have manifested such an amazing life for myself. I am a Yoga Teacher, certified Women's Empowerment Coach, and International Speaker. I get to help other women find their sparkle again and inspire them to chase their dreams. I get invited to speak around the world to audiences of women who want to change their lives. I throw conscious, sober dance parties, and am part of an awakened community in Sydney filled with high-vibe humans who are doing things to raise the collective consciousness of the globe. I wake up every day so incredibly grateful, and love who I see when I look in the mirror.

At the time of writing this, I am one year alcohol-free. I no longer feel like I am living a double life – the Big Jourdi pulses through me and I do things to stay connected to her daily, like nature walks, meditation, ocean swims, breathwork, and yoga. I travel the world, speaking at events and running my coaching business online. Just as the voice told me in the car that morning, putting the drink down has made room for all my dreams to come true.

I have come full circle to realize that drugs, alcohol, sex, status, money, relationships, and luxury were never going to fill my cup. I have learned that no matter what you have in life materialistically, everything you need to be fulfilled lives within. It's about tapping into that space and accessing that part of yourself. When you are living your truth, in alignment with your soul's purpose, One Big Energy brings all the necessary opportunities to you that will assist you in flourishing and living a life of abundance. Not the financial, superficial abundance – but that deep, true, soul-level abundance where everything just flows. The fairy with broken wings has found her power and transformed into the goddess who soars.

If my story resonates with you, or you are struggling with addiction, stop right now. Put your hand over your heart and close your eyes. Take deep breaths. Feel your power that lives inside of you; it's right there under your palms. Whisper to yourself, "I love you, I am listening." Then have the courage to hear what your soul needs and take action based on that, it won't lead you astray. If I can do it, so can you darling.

Maritta Philp

Belmar Therapy

https://www.linkedin.com/in/maritta-philp-7648a5125/
https://www.facebook.com/belmartherapy
https://consciousrelationships.com

Dr. Maritta Philp is a much sought-after transformational coach and therapist with a focus on helping her clients create extraordinary relationships with themselves, others, and life itself. One of her passions is to support her clients in their awakening, facilitating experiences of deep peace, love, and connection.

She started her career as a General Practitioner but moved into coaching and therapy over 15 years ago, having overcome her own struggles with childhood trauma and co-dependence. She is a successful author, having previously published two books.

Maritta combines traditional and ancient techniques in her approach.

Today, when she's not walking her dog, reading, or writing, you'll often find her helping her clients on their journey of empowerment, especially around re-parenting younger parts of themselves and what it takes to have amazing relationships.

To learn more about Maritta and how she can help you grow beyond your trauma, visit: mp.marittaphilp.com.

CHANGING (ELEVATING) PERSPECTIVES

By Maritta Philp

Trauma leads to the loss of yourself. It leads to a fracturing of the self and a disconnection from who you really are. It is not only what happened to you, but your reaction to what happened. It is what you had to do to survive, the false meaning you arrived at about who and what you are. Whilst this might sound like a one-way street, in truth it is not. There is hope. There is always hope.

There is so much I would like to tell you, so much to share, and not enough words to say it all. So let me begin by telling you a little bit about my own life, the trauma I lived through, what I learned through it all, and the blessings that were bestowed upon me because of this.

We human beings are a social species. We don't do well without connection and belonging. These truly are core human needs. Infants will die without love, care, and connection, even if they are cared for physically.

I am the second child in my family. Due to a difference in blood types, my mother's immune system produced antibodies against both my older brother's and my blood while in the womb. As a result, when I was born, I was very anaemic and incredibly unwell. I was rushed off to intensive care and received several whole blood exchanges and remained in hospital for about three weeks. During that era, quite a few decades ago, parents were not allowed to be with their baby at all and all my mother could do when visiting was to stare at me through a glass window, lying alone in a crib.

The only way for an infant to connect is through physical touch. A baby needs to be held and comforted to deal with overwhelming emotions such as fear. I have no conscious memory of these weeks in the hospital, and I can only imagine the fear and the pain that went along with this experience.

I was pricked by needles, exposed to the harsh light of an intensive care unit and loud noises, and subjected to the emotional intensity of a whole team of doctors and nurses encroaching upon me, violating my physical body, literally piercing all my boundaries with no ability for me to do anything about it or protect myself. I experienced a complete lack of safety while being separated from my mother. I experienced this not just for a day or two, but for weeks.

And they saved my life. I am very grateful for this. It is just a shame that during that time little was known about the impact of traumatic experiences of this kind. Because whilst they were busy saving my life, I must have felt I was dying, overwhelmed and traumatised. And although I have no conscious memory of this time, the aftereffects are with me to this day, in every breath and in every heartbeat, colouring the way I view the world on a deep and profound level.

Even as I am thinking about this now, it feels as though it happened to someone else, not me. This is what I mean when I mention disconnection and shattering of the self. This experience was so overwhelming and painful, the only thing I could do was to disconnect from this part of me.

Most families are complicated—mine was no different. I lived with my older brother, my parents, and my father's aunt. My great aunt had lived with my father before my mother even met him. It can't have been easy for my mother to move into this constellation. There must have been competition between both women to care for my father and competition for his attention. I don't really know whether this contributed to him being emotionally absent. The fact remains that he chose to not be there for his children. He made lots of promises he never kept. The only way to get any sort of approval was through good grades—needing to be perfect, keeping up an image to impress others.

Then, one day, my relationship to life took another huge blow. I must have been about 10 or 11 years old. I can't remember my age exactly, but I was a bubbly young girl who loved to dance and skip around. I came into the lounge where my dad was sitting on the couch on his own. I was dancing around, singing, being filled with joy—being unselfconsciously me. I cannot remember if any words were spoken. Suddenly, my dad got up and left the room. He went into the garden and as I was watching him go, I could see the expression on his face change. His face became a grimace of disgust and hatred. He couldn't wait to get away from me. I remember the feeling like it happened yesterday. I was deflated, crushed, devastated. I sank onto that couch like all my joy, all my life-force, had been sucked out of my body. At this moment I made a decision. Never again would I allow anyone to see who I truly was. The conception I came to about myself was that I was disgusting, unlikable, and if I was truly me, people would leave.

Some years later my dad was having an affair and my parents divorced. I was 15 years old when we moved out. The divorce proceedings were heard before a court with my father stating that he didn't want me. He made no claim as a father, didn't ask for visiting rights or wanted anything to do with me. By that time the belief that I was unwanted was a big part of my identity.

I wish someone had been able to explain to me when I was younger that none of the things my father said or did had anything to do with me; that I was a loveable girl, with so many gifts and beautiful qualities. I wish they had told me that my father's words and actions were simply an expression of his own pain, his own limiting beliefs, his own trauma he had never worked through.

But no one told me. And so, for most of my existence I experienced life and myself as partial, disconnected, and fractured. There was no wholeness, no peace, and though I was very much loved by my mother, I wasn't able to feel her love. For many years I felt I had no right to even be alive. "Excuse me for being alive" was a common thought. I was thinking about death and dying every single day for decades. Of course, I wouldn't share this with anyone. The thought of being this vulnerable triggered a fear deep within the essence of my being. I associated vulnerability with helplessness, being overwhelmed, and annihilation.

The meaning I had arrived at about myself and life was diminishing and restrictive. "I am all alone," "I am powerless," and "I am not safe" were some of the most common thoughts. Perhaps the deepest of them all was "I am unwanted."

The beliefs I came to about who I was and the resulting actions have cost me dearly. Self-harming, ending up in a sexually abusive relationship in my 20s, and feeling disconnected from everything and everyone are just some examples. I was betrayed and abandoned by my best friend. Life felt impossible. I just wanted to leave.

But I don't want to paint my life as having been totally miserable; that would neither be fair, nor true. I had the most amazing experiences on my journey of healing, I met the most extraordinary people, and can now look back at all my trauma and see it as a gift. It has always been something that happened for me, and not to me. It has helped me to awaken.

And this single word changed everything. It happened for me, not to me. If this was true, what would that mean? How could I now perceive myself and life through this different lens? On the most basic level it allowed me to shift away from victimhood, from feeling helpless to empowered, from feeling alone and abandoned to being part of something extraordinary.

Let me be very clear, this is not about excusing abusive behaviour or minimising the pain I was in. This is about making a shift in perception. Because without this shift, being a victim is all I could ever be.

Words carry incredible power. With the thoughts I think and the words I use, fuelled by emotions that go along with them, I create my experience of the present moment and determine the trajectory of my life. Just think about a ship's journey across the ocean prior to modern technology. The course had to be set and being just half a degree off would mean arriving in a totally different destination, or not arriving at all. The longer the journey, the greater the distance from the set destination.

Let me give you a personal example. Deep sadness and feeling alone has been a big part of my life. This can be expressed in a variety of ways. I can say, "I am sad" or I can say, "In this moment there is a part of me that feels sad." I invite you to say both sentences out loud and notice the difference in how you feel saying either sentence. Do you notice the huge difference? Of course, I don't want to lie to myself, I can't simply say "I am happy" when I feel sad. But how I express the truth has a huge impact. Anything we preface with "I am" is incredibly powerful. This is about our identity, who we are. And whatever or whoever we identify as is at the steering wheel of our life.

When I say, "I am sad" I become that sadness. I identify with the sadness. It seems an all-encompassing and timeless truth. When I say, "In this moment there is a part of me that feels sad" there is a more spaciousness for things to be different in the next moment, and for other parts of me to not feel sad.

For me, the response to my trauma has directed my life for many decades. Out of "I am all alone" grew someone who felt left out, unsupported, and unable to ask for help. "I am powerless" produced someone who wouldn't speak up, who felt hopeless, depressed, and obsessed with dying. "I am not safe" created a people pleaser, someone who has been co-dependent for most of her life.

This might sound very depressing, but there is good news. None of those statements are actually true. These were all strategies I employed to survive. And the same is true for you. Whatever you are making your trauma mean about you has helped you to survive. But is it helping you anymore? Or is it keeping you stuck in the past, keeping you from creating the life you wish to lead? Is the meaning you are making here true?

The biggest gift I received from the trauma was the ability to go within. The outside world felt harsh and scary to me, so I went on a quest to explore my inner universe. I wanted to get better; I wanted to heal. I wanted my life to be beautiful and meaningful. I wanted to be able to look back over my life at the very end and be proud of a life well lived. So I began this extraordinary journey of healing and integration.

I explored my unconscious beliefs and thought patterns. I learned how powerful my identity is in creating certain experiences and these experiences provided proof that what I believed was true, even when it wasn't. I had to come to terms with me being the one who was ultimately responsible for my own experiences. There truly was no one to blame.

I began to grow up. I became an adult in the truest sense of the word for the first time in my life, a n adult able to hold those fractured parts within myself. I learned to reparent all the younger selves still very much alive within me that were throwing tantrums, running away scared, hiding, feeling alone and left out. I no longer allowed my 3-year-old self to drive the bus, but had her securely strapped into the child seat and I, the adult, was now at the steering wheel of my life.

I learned to become the observer of inner experience. I experienced my true self to be aware. And just like you can project any film on the screen in the movie theatre without the screen ever being damaged, I learned that no matter what happened in my life, the truth of who I am can never be damaged. I still get triggered and identify with traumatised parts of myself, but it is happening less and less.

The gift of the trauma is my awakening. To touch something divine and eternal for which there are no words. The gift of my trauma is deep tenderness, love, and compassion for myself and others. The gift of my trauma is poetry. I would like to leave you with a poem I have written and to know that wherever you are on this journey, you are not alone. You are loved.

The Threshold

I am teetering on the threshold, with the doorway right there, right in front of me.

I see the joy, love, and freedom on the other side as I glance through the doorway.

I see green meadows, people laughing, children playing, the sun glistening on clear water.

I only allow myself to take a little peek, held back by enormous forces, staying in the shadows of the life that is possible for me.

I know once I am on the other side, I will be free.

Yet I choose to remain where I am.

Old beliefs, old ties, old resentments, false loyalties, and toxic love forming a powerful web that keeps me entangled, enmeshed, stuck and unable to make my move.

Aeons pass by. Lives full of regret and sorrow. Always staying in the shadows.

Until one day I choose differently.

It is time. The time is now. I take a deep breath, and with my eyes wide open, I make my move, leaving behind the illusion, the fear, the doubt, and the darkness.

None of the old can make it through this doorway, the old cocoon in which I was living my life stripped away as I step into the truth of who I am.

And I understand the deeper truth that even in the darkness, living in the shadows, it was me all along who held myself there; the darkness enabling me to see the blazing light I truly am.

For I am Truth. I am Goodness. I am Grace. I am Beauty. I am Freedom. I am Love.

Naomi Gobits

Victim to Victory & Feel to Heal
Coach

https://www.linkedin.com/in/naomi-gobits-73b834b5/
https://www.facebook.com/gobits/
https://www.instagram.com/alohahealing8/

My name is Naomi Gobits. I have been in the healing and health industry for 28 years. I was a massage therapist for 25 years working in various 5-star day spas and worked with a chiropractor as well. I loved anything about the body as it has so much wisdom. I then went on to study an amazing modality called holographic kinetics, a timeline therapy that helps to remove trauma from the timeline to match the mind with the body, as so many people have problems that stem from the mind. I now love to help others empower themselves to see the gift in their past, take back their power, and gain a fulfilled life. Blessings to you.

VICTIM TO VICTORY: FEEL TO HEAL

By Naomi Gobits

A tribute to my beautiful sister, may she rest in peace. Thank you for teaching me so many amazing lessons and giving me so many gifts.

Feel to Heal

This is my story of how I overcame my sister's death in 2005. I hope this can help other people who have been or are going through a similar experience. May my words touch your mind, heart, and body. Enjoy the journey.

I will never forget the day I went to see my sister for the last time in the hospital. She had been battling a brain tumour for three years, had headaches daily, and felt sick every day. She had eventually fallen out of bed, had a stroke, and was left with left-side paralysis.

The tumour was at the back of the cerebellum, which is the part of the brain located at the back of the head, just above and behind where the spinal cord connects to the brain itself. It was operated on once by a well-known surgeon in Sydney, claiming to be the only doctor who could go where no other would. This operation helped a little bit, but the tumour grew back aggressively and my sister went back to the hospital.

I remember her saying, "I need to be washed and dressed," to the nurse as she sat up in bed. I felt she knew that she would be GOING soon, and she was getting ready. My heart sank; it was such a strong gut feeling that I couldn't ignore it. I said to her, "Ok, I am going to go now," knowing it would be the last time I saw her.

She said to me, "I will see you again someday, follow your dreams, and live life to the fullest." I smiled through my tears and heartache and said, "Yes, I will see you again one day. Love you always."

That night, as I sat at home crying uncontrollably, I heard, "What do I do if I see the white light?" (I could hear my sister saying, "It's called clairaudient.") I replied, "GO to it, go to it," and sang the song *Ascension* by Sacred Earth. She passed that night. My body felt numb, my heart felt intense pain, and my mind couldn't grasp or process that she was really gone. To this day, I hate saying goodbye to people. I cried for weeks, isolating myself in my home. My closest friend was gone, and who would I be without her? I would do anything for her. We knew each other so deeply that sometimes we didn't need to talk, we just *knew*.

This was the beginning of the unravelling and of me trying to pick up the pieces of my broken heart to comfort myself. I started eating. Food was the beginning of my new addiction. I knew that I was depressed, and the only thing that helped temporarily was food. I felt helpless and it seemed like I was in a rotation of grief, sadness, disbelief, frustration, and anger that God had taken my sister away. I was angry at myself for not being able to save her, my ego trying desperately to grab onto something to avoid the heartache.

I finally received some counselling and new tools to deal with my feelings as I felt so sad. At one point, I didn't want to be here by myself anymore. I had hit rock bottom, I felt, and it was time I sought support. I knew the only way to go was UP, and I needed to support myself and make a change. I had a choice: avoid the pain or feel it and heal it. I chose to avoid it for a bit longer until my unconscious eating got out of hand. I had to help myself; no one else could do it for me.

I had thrown myself into work as a massage therapist, working at five-day spas, doing about twenty-five massages a week. When I arrived home, I'd feel exhausted and I'd push through my pain, further disconnecting myself from it. My mind wanted to be busy, running around doing things so I would not feel. Just when I thought I had it all sorted out, a client would come into work and ask out of the blue, "So do you have a sister?"

I began sharing some of my story. It was a big pill to swallow, as some people don't know how to deal with death. It's a huge personal journey that is different for everyone. Some people, like me, avoid their pain and 'get on with life'. In my case, it took a while. I spent a good ten years continuing to avoid my pain before I began sorting through my unconscious eating habits and depression and started to reconnect to my feelings, taking back my life that had been consumed by this situation.

Then, once I started to notice my thoughts spiral down and up again, I decided it was a GIFT. I asked myself, "What can this teach me about myself?" A light bulb moment. I knew there was a choice to either keep going down the rabbit hole or accept just what IS and make friends with my emotions. I called my sadness 'BLUE'—just a feeling that travels through me. I cry, soothe myself, and then I'm back to being myself. I applied this every day and it helped me move through my emotions with more ease.

One day at work, I was exhausted. I just couldn't give anymore. I had adrenal fatigue from pushing myself and not giving myself time to just be. It happened because I'd neglected my health and I needed to find balance. So, I took the next year off work, replenishing my health, finding some balance in my body through massages and acupuncture, and seeing a counsellor. Body, mind, and spirit were all being attended to. I filled my cup once again and my self-pity started to shift into self-love. I put myself first, tending to my inner garden.

I'd ask myself, "What would it feel like if I just accepted this?" I couldn't bring her back; her body wasn't healthy and she'd wanted to go. I couldn't heal her, it wasn't my job, and she chose to go. So, it was time to let go and release the guilt of not being able to save her. BREATHE. This is a gift that I have learned about myself. It is who I am and what I have become, and I will never give up on myself. I see and feel the gift or – to put it another way – the positive or negative outcome to a situation. I know it is a choice to stay in a dark well or climb my way out, supporting myself all the way. I realised I was strong, and while I never gave up on myself, I almost did before choosing to shift my mindset. When I self-soothed, I'd tell myself, "It's ok, just feel this, breathe into your stomach, and this too shall pass. This is just energy in motion, so FLIP THE FEELING and be kind to yourself. Mother yourself."

I had wanted to rescue my sister, but the person who needed rescuing was me, to bring myself back to wholeness. It began to feel like the beginning of the journey back to my authentic self. I had to let go of control and get out of my own way, being the observer of my emotions, feeling them but not attaching any story to them. I learned to SURRENDER and let go, a cliché but true nevertheless, and it took me a long time, believe me! As each day passed, I chose to make friends with death, with my old beliefs and limitations, and open to expansion and acceptance and finally peace. It is a never-ending process, as you don't really ever stop unravelling, and peace doesn't happen overnight. It has taken me seventeen years to share my story, and I still shed tears remembering my sister, but I don't regret a second of my journey.

Every year on 28 January, the anniversary of my sister's death, I still cry for her, feel sad, and miss her physically, but the pain has lessened, and my heartache has dissipated into self-acceptance. I am no longer angry with God for taking her away. For a long time, I wanted to blame someone and I was angry with the surgeon who operated on her tumour, until I realised it was purely about my own choices to turn the situation away from being a victim and coming out the other side to VICTORY with the wisdom to share my story. I have learned strength and perseverance and that everything I seek is inside of me, that my mind, my body, can do anything. I have found that if I avoid my feelings it can turn into rage, days of depression and exhaustion, and I become out of balance and out of control. If someone triggers me emotionally, I explode and then feel guilty.

My advice is just to BREATHE big breaths into your stomach, ground yourself, and even giggle a bit to bypass the ego. I choose to own my triggers. I choose to seek truth and freedom in various modalities to increase my emotional toolset. In addition to massage and acupuncture, I have had kinesiology sessions and recently spinal flow sessions to feel the deeper layers of my old traumas that I hadn't processed. These emotional, physical, and chemical stressors were stored in my spine, as I didn't know how to process them at the time. With this modality, I could feel the stress release and feel myself come into a space of ease and peace instead of emotional overwhelm. By helping yourself emotionally, you also support yourself physically, as the body shifts through layers; the spiritual, the mental, the emotional, and finally the physical body itself. The lesson is then understood. Swimming is also helpful in releasing stress and allowing you to come into energetic alignment.

Once you have embodied all the information, you will be able to support anyone you meet – a client, a partner, a friend you meet in the street – who shares that their sister has just passed away. As I said before, death is completely different for everyone, it's not a race to the finish line, it's an unravelling of self-discovery. The old stagnant beliefs, ancestral or past life, to new understandings and beliefs, have allowed me to be sovereign and heal my heart and mind and overcome many obstacles. I have left the blame game behind and now take responsibility for my emotions and feelings. I hope that sharing my story here will shed some light on other people who have gone through a similar experience. Many people find this a hard topic to talk about, so why not find the inner healer within? As clichéd as this is, there is light at the end of the tunnel and that light is YOU. I am grateful for all the lessons I have learned; I am grateful for understanding what death taught me. Life is about choice; no matter what you choose, choose LIFE.

I am grateful for the experiences I have been through; I have healed my eating imbalances, which showed me I was stuffing down my emotions instead of feeling them; my mind is balanced as is my physical body. My journey right now is to love and to choose to be empowered in every situation.

Each experience shows you a deeper lesson, and by breaking through those ancestral limitations you find more peace, more empowerment, more love for yourself. I truly believe that everything heals. It just depends on which way you look at it and feel it.

Thank you for taking the time to read my story. I hope it has touched your heart and your mind and brought more peace to your soul.

Ny Young

HA! Sessions
Holistic Creative Coach

https://www.facebook.com/profile.php?id=100016227187206
https://tl.page/hasessions
https://spotify.link/QKMz7nRi7Cb

Ny is a trained gospel, contemporary, and classical singer. She's also an actress who's worked in the industry for over 20 years teaching and working on community projects, and has appeared in several small screen/off-broadway stints. She's currently the host of a faith-based podcast, KoffeeSipsTea, where she chats about entrepreneurship, holistic healthcare, and creativity all with a kingdom twist. This is on Apple and Spotify. Ny is also a Holistic Creative Coach of HA! Sessions to unlock unlimited creativity. You may also follow Ny on Twitter @HaSessions123 or FB @HoneyNy Ny for more updates.

FINDING CREATIVE PURPOSE THROUGH FINDING MY FAITH

By Ny Young

Introduction

Picture a young woman in her 20s getting out of a cab in an urban city mixed with southern hospitality. This woman is oozing with confidence, excitement, and a little bit of nervousness, embarking on a new adventure to fulfill her career. This woman is me, beginning a long journey to finding creative purpose through spiritual health and wellness. On this day, however, while taking in the view of concrete buildings and bustling L trains, my only belief was in fulfilling the American dream of white picket fences and 2.5-bedroom houses. My dream of getting into a graduate program was the proverbial checkmark on my list of many career goals to complete. Then, suddenly everything began to unravel, leading to complete brokenness. If a seemingly brilliant woman like me was crushing their goals, how did everything spiral into a world full of numbness, void of any meaningful connections?

Trying to fill the Void

My life took on a routine of busyness, attending classes full time, writing papers late into the night, and then falling asleep in a fit of exhaustion, only to do this all over again the next day. In addition to attending classes full-time, going to a volunteer center once a week, and working part-time on weekends, my daily commute robbed me of my remaining energy. There was hardly any time left to rest or have a social life. Although my schedule was full, my heart still was very empty. While trying to fill the void of emptiness, my first thought during this season was to look for a creative outlet. So, acting classes it was! They were added to my task list as an ode to my formative years. Even though the people were great in my acting classes, getting up every week for training felt like a chore and still didn't fill the void of unmet needs. These unmet needs included the longing for a family of my own, meaningful social connections, to feel understood, and to finally be at peace. My health also began to deteriorate around this time, making the anguish of being in a new city while transitioning into adulthood that much harder to navigate. My classmates seemed alienated by my social withdrawal and my teachers appeared to be quite dismissive of my painful silence. After having a talk with the department chair, it was mutually decided that a leave of absence would be best. Once in the presence of family, everything seemed to improve. Tender-Loving-Care seemed to be the answer to life on the brink of an existential crisis and a nervous breakdown. In the "city that never sleeps," seeing old friends, going to social gatherings, and eating all the cultural flavors of different cuisines at any given time, became a consolation, soothing a home-sick young woman like myself. Also, hearing animated stories from friends whispering late into the night, became the icing on my slice of buttercream cake. Soon, it was time to head back to the urban city of southern hospitality. This time, however, the strange city would seem a bit more familiar.

Back in a Strange Place

Once back in classes, my grades soared. The leave of absence had worked! Until, the feelings of uneasiness began to return. So, the following semester, my graduate studies came to an abrupt stop. Soon, the search for purpose began while being unemployed without savings, feeling destitute, burnt out, exhausted, stagnant, and overwhelmed with daily life. A quarter-life crisis was on the horizon when something began to stir in me. It was during that time of wading through the urban jungle, looking for another job opportunity, that God began to minister to my heart. My faith was being stirred in my spirit, growing stronger each day and my spirit was longing to be known by someone. That someone was my Higher Power beckoning me to, "Acknowledge

Him in all things so that He would direct my paths"(Pro 3:6). Thus, began my spiritual reawakening to dive into my faith journey.

Walk by Faith

After some soul searching, prayer, meditation, and yes, even more training (this included completing my Master's degree and becoming a certified coach), Most High developed my coaching program.

During this soul care adventure, there were many twists and turns to develop my coaching program as a Holistic Creative Coach. Providing HA! Sessions would give clients Kingdom Creative Strategies to improve their overall quality of life through interactive lessons while giving glory to God.

Keeping my faith front and center allowed me to become a Holistic Creative Coach. Walking out my faith, also allowed me to keep my creative muscles active working in TV, film, and theatre, traveling throughout the United States to find faith, staying connected to ministry and family members while eating nourishing food, supporting my spiritual journey, and finally leading to freedom at home.

Sustaining Peace

Despite past nay-sayers, my life is ok. I'm at peace, and now I'm supporting others in their creative journeys that also bring them peace. As the Bible scripture says in 2 Cor 5:7, "We walk by faith and not by sight," which has become one of my favorite affirming scriptures.

Based on my faith, background in performing arts, personal experience, and certification in coaching, my approach to supporting others is on the holistic side. Spirituality, one of our primary resources of nourishment, is the main focus of my coaching practice. People tap into their unlimited creative potential through whole-body integration, connecting mind, body, and spirit. With the holistic approach, people then have a way to connect spiritual health and wellness to their creative pursuits from a place of peace. HA! Sessions create a safe positive environment to gain clarity and discover one's creative prowess while having fun through customized courses.

I've built meaningful connections with some of my clients and even interviewed some of them on my Faith-based podcast, KoffeeSipsTea. On this podcast, we celebrate Creativepreneurs, local artisans, Spiritual Health, and wellness from a Kingdom perspective. My small clientele have aced their projects and continue to get better every day. Their creative pursuits range from self-taught production to journeying abroad as travel aficionados. My clients' creative potential is unlimited as they realize they have the full backing of the Most High God. I've learned to accept that Most High has a purpose for all of our lives, and it's up to us to discover this purpose. He is the Great Physician with the Great Prescription for abundant, whole-body living.

How to Discover Your Creative Purpose

One thing that I've learned in my spiritual faith journey with the Creator God is that we are blessed with the gift of creativity. As creatives "We are His masterpiece" (Eph 2:10), placed on this Earth to share our creative gifts with others. While not everyone may share the same beliefs as mine, that's ok. All faiths are welcome, after all, to my sessions. I've always shared my faith during these Spirit-led sessions since 2017, and everyone took away something different each time. These HA! sessions were able to help others who needed confidence, a common challenge among workshop attendees, by discovering their Kingdom purpose. During these sessions, we simply discovered what was in our hands and homes with available tools already at our fingertips. Through this process, we defeated our limiting beliefs, rebuilt our skill sets regardless of knowledge or skill levels, dealt with self-sabotaging behaviors, and moved into a spiritual place of abundance, receptive to God's will for our abundant lives!

Lessons Learned

Some of the lessons learned during this past decade as a continuous learner were to:

Be open to new opportunities.

Stand firm on personal truths.

Rejection is an opportunity for our protection and sometimes leads to redirection.

The possibilities are endless.

Creative performance is as easy as breathing.

Expressing gratitude maximizes abundance.

Maintain social connections whenever possible.

The glass is neither half full nor half empty, but overflowing with blessings.

Keep Faith first by taking that leap! With God by our side all things are possible (Mat 19:26).

Nourishing relationships through SoulCare is spiritual self-care.

Take care of your instrument and your instrument will take care of you.

Trust God's process (It's God's character development).

Your tests and trials will lead to your testimony.

We are a work in progress!

God has got this! He will meet us where we are! So let's rest in His promises.

Conclusion

My main mission and purpose as a Holistic Creative Coach is to meet others where they are in life, at my coffee table, while giving God the glory! This involves bridging the gap between different learning styles, creative performance, and daily life commitments. These sessions all rely heavily on a biblical application since the word of God is life and love-affirming in my humble opinion. Through interactive courses called HA! sessions, whole body integration is possible in as little as 30 seconds a day over a 10-week period to improve the client's overall quality of life. We also use the N.O.S.H. SM method, which stands for Nourish our Soul Health, personally developed after realizing that many creative professionals seem to neglect their spiritual and physical health. We use this method to assess our spiritual health and wellness temperatures throughout the day. Through the seven stages of the N.O.S.H. SM method, which include praying, breathing, watering our gardens, resting, and nourishing our bodies with real whole food ingredients, we can improve our lifestyles. We are more like gardens and not machines, which means that whatever is sowed into us will be reaped during harvest season. It is my belief that our thought life, physical health, creativity, and spirituality are all interconnected, leading to improvement in our overall quality of life when we nourish our spiritual health. This spiritual awareness leads to balance when we recognize that we are already equipped with many intangible gifts such as encouragement, prayer, love, joy, empowerment, empathy, and patience. We can't help but share our many blessings with others once we are aware of our spiritual wealth. By building these engagements, we create a positive alliance.

Through my assistance, others are able to receive access to tools that weren't available to me during my early adolescence while overcoming a mindset of insecurity and scarcity. With my coaching methods, others now have an opportunity to go from creative restlessness to creative strategic goal-keeping from a place of rest. Then they will remain in the creative overflow of abundance!

Because there isn't a shortage of creative ideas…creativity is infinite!

I'm thankful to God for wanting to use me as an instrument to share His blessings with others. He thought enough of little ole' me to do the unimaginable. By saying yes to God and partnering with Him, He has activated my faith. This has resulted in radical generosity, expressions of gratitude, and accelerated growth with an overflow of abundance to many community members. He has brought me many breakthroughs from being on the verge of many breakdowns. His undeserved grace continues to motivate me to share my faith with others about Jesus. People then become aware of His Kingdom Creative Lifestyle, combining wellness with worship, leading to faith combined with fitness.

As the host of the Honey Lattes VIP Community, we recently had our second annual SoulCare: HA! Coaching Program for women in May 2023 centered around relationships. This program led to a SoulCare Abundance 10-week guided prayer and journaling event requested by popular demand. This experience taught me that prayer, praise, and purposeful planning lead to fruitful action. I'm grateful to all the women who took part in this series!

Currently, I'm running a virtual, one-year Bible study for women that takes followers from Genesis to Revelation. My hope is for others to challenge their beliefs when it comes to the word and their understanding of God to better relate to Him during their creative pursuits.

Thank you for reading my chapter, and I'm praying that the reader is encouraged to take a small actionable step towards one transformative life goal. I'm always available if you would like a listening ear and as always through prayer; God is only a call away.

Penny Watson

Penny Ann
Author

https://www.facebook.com/PennyAnn
https://authorpennyann.com/

Canadian-born author Penny Ann faced her own personal struggles, including battling cancer, and took control of her life making conscious choices that led her on a path of self-discovery and healing. Penny experienced a profound reconnection and felt she had to share her God-given vision with the world. During the pandemic of 2020, she did just that by publishing her first novel, *Peddlers*, a prophetic vision written in the eighties that will take you on an adventure you will not soon forget. Driven by her unyielding passion for storytelling and spiritual insights, Penny made the bold decision to leave behind her forty-four-year waitressing career and fully focus on her writing and personal growth. Now, she is a successful international best-selling author of three books, *Peddlers, Havanna,* and *The Dreamspellers*. Penny's transformative tales continue to inspire and empower her readers to embark on their own journeys of self-discovery and enlightenment.

IT WAS TIME FOR A NEW ME!

By Penny Watson

I was born and raised in Montreal, Canada with an identical twin sister, Candy, with whom I was very connected right from the start. We shared dreams, completed each other's sentences, exchanged conscious awareness, and felt each other's pain both physically and emotionally. I grew up not knowing that I was psychic and thought everyone had the ability to connect to God and to other people.

My first clear message from God came to me at the age of five. He said that I was here to be a witness for him during the time of the apocalypse/revelations/rapture. He said not to worry as I would be old by then, grandma age. I look at it now as the time of the ascension. My relationship with God was very personal to me, and I did not feel a need to share it with anyone else, not even my twin.

I told God then that I wanted to live to be a hundred years old and that if I were to have any illnesses or ailments, could I have them while I was young and strong and not when I was old? I had no idea what that would mean physically, emotionally, or mentally, but I was about to find out.

At fourteen, God came to me during a time when I was feeling self-conscious and he told me that I would meet my husband later in life and that he would be much older than I was. He would have been married before and have two sons. His name would start with a "J." I never forgot that over the years, looking in vain for the elusive "J."

By this time, I recognized that some of my dreams were coming true to the smallest detail up to twelve years after having them. I tried to hide the fact that I was different. I always knew people's inner thoughts but trained myself not to pay attention as people did not like me in their heads. I considered it cheating when it came to games and cards.

I felt that if I did more for others, then they would love me. Then I could be lovable and maybe even learn to love myself.

As a teenager, a twin, and an empath, I had a difficult time discerning who I really was. I was constantly looking outside of myself for validation. I felt others knew better than I did, not realizing it was a lack of trust in God and myself. This sent me down a path of self-discovery. I walked away from the hypocrisy of my religion and started to learn about more esoteric understandings such as reincarnation and Karma. My twin, Candy, became born again. Believe me, we had our fights over the years, but we were both trying to understand the gift that had been bestowed upon us.

I had many health problems from an early age, ignoring injuries from sports and just plain clumsiness. As well as experiencing blood poisoning twice, hypothermia, and many dental issues, I injured my tailbone, ankle, back, and neck in separate accidents. I must come from a tougher time because I never complained or made a fuss over such things. It was, after all, part of my agreement with God.

I had my first operation to remove a seven-inch in diameter cyst at nineteen, followed by cancer at twenty-one, which came back while I was still doing ongoing treatments. My commitment to spiritual understanding increased at this time. After all, why would God tell me he had a plan for me and then make me so sick? It would be over thirty-five years before I would understand that it was to teach me to love myself.

By 1983, I saw my cancer as a wake-up call from God to clean up my life from all the traumas that I had experienced. I was tired of having my heart broken time and again. I came to understand that I was picking up too much negative energy from others and adopting their pain as my own. Because I had no outlet, it was causing a disease within me.

By my mid-twenties, I was experiencing pain in my hip and back and was erroneously given a lift for the wrong shoe. Within the year, I was crippled. That started a year of traction three times a week on my neck, back, and hips. By my late twenties, the doctors said I was looking at a wheelchair, and that I would never run again. Did they have any idea of the impact that would have on me?

I became determined, at that time, to rejoin softball the next year just because they said I could never run again. I am stubborn that way. I learned how to swim and worked my way up to swimming a mile a day within a year. I started cycling and building up my muscles after years of atrophy. Did I still have pain? You have no idea!

I lived through the worst pain of my life during the late eighties, but it led me to an understanding that pain and suffering were two different things. If I focused on the pain, my life was unbearable. If I focused on what gave me joy, the suffering went away. I became more compassionate toward others and their daily struggles. We all have our crosses to bear.

I went down some dark roads and thoughts at that time. I was in a dark place without hope or a vision of myself having a future. I was in despair! I longed to find my way back to the light. Just knowing there was light, love, and peace out there somewhere, kept me from making even worse mistakes. I turned away from hopelessness and reconnected with my higher self. It was at this time that I wrote my first novel, *Peddlers,* which I never published.

I experienced many spiritual gifts at this time that strengthened my relationship with God. My mind-reading abilities came back to me as well as channeling His words upon the page. I had no idea then what it was called; I only knew how wonderful I felt while in those meditative states. It was at this time that I started to receive messages from God. Most of the time, they were for me, but many times, the messages were for other people.

I spent the next dozen years learning about spiritual things, chakras, meditation, astrology, and card reading. This was a point of great dissension between Candy and I. She believed that if it was not from the Bible, it was from the devil. I believed that this was the means that God chose to reach me. Luckily, our love was stronger than our opinions.

I stopped listening to most music at this time as the 440 Hz frequency that has been the cornerstone of our music industry is not a harmonic frequency. I reduced my social circles and even filtered the books that I was reading to ones that were uplifting. I learned to say "no" for the first time in my life and to know that it was ok to do so. People would still like me.

By the year 2000, I had decided to live my life consciously, not reactively. I had just come out of an abusive relationship and was very depressed. I was an easy target for those whose intentions were not pure. When I realized that depression was anger turned inward, I stopped being mad at myself and started taking full responsibility for everything that had ever happened to me. I learned that I can not change what I have not owned up to. I had to forgive myself for living my life reactively from subconscious programming and start making conscious decisions in my life, for my life. Then, things started to change. I started to love myself, but I withdrew too much away from others to protect my precious new ideas lest they be dashed.

I met my husband, Paul, in 2001, not knowing he was the man that God told me about when I was fourteen. He was fifteen years older than I, and I was now in my late thirties, but his name was Paul, and he only had one son. He did not fully fit the criteria. It was three years into the relationship when he revealed to me that he did in fact have two sons. Then it dawned on me that his full name was John Paul. After that, I never doubted for a second that this was the man that God knew would make me happy. We were a perfect match.

Over the course of the next seven years, I started having stomach problems which turned out to be excess acid from a hiatus hernia. Due to heavy bleeding all my life, I became anemic and had to have a hysterectomy. Two years later, just after breaking my nose, I discovered that I had breast cancer followed by many bouts of diverticulitis. Did I really want to live to be a hundred? A change in diet was called for.

Life became very happy and peaceful after that up until my husband passed away in September 2019 from stage four lung cancer. God came to me and comforted me when I found out that Paul had two months left to live. He revealed to me that he was moving my feet onto a new path, and Paul was one of the things that had to go. In His wisdom, He did not reveal, at that time, that it would all have to go. I was not ready to hear that yet.

I found myself in complete solitude for two years. I mourned for six months, and then the pandemic hit, further secluding me at home. Listening to my inner voice was the only thing that sustained me at this time. It was then that I reconnected to Source Consciousness and made new decisions for my life in partnership with God. The message to "love myself" was getting louder.

Although Candy and I have always been close, the pandemic drew us closer as we both had the exact same thoughts and feelings regarding it. We could clearly see then that God was indeed reaching me with His words, but in a different fashion than how He was reaching Candy. The important thing was that we were both listening. God be praised!

I decided to pick up my writing again when I found my book, *Peddlers*, buried in storage while purging the house. I had written *Peddlers* in 1987, later transcribing it onto the computer, and then ended up burying it for over 30 years. After the pandemic started in 2020, I realized that the back history of my book was starting to come true. It was then that I knew that *Peddlers* had to be published. I took two hundred pages out of the original novel, including the back history of the story, and started trying to figure out how to get it published.

During one of my conversations with God, I lamented that if He was moving my feet upon a new path, then why was nothing happening? Why was I still stuck at home alone, working the same job, and having no friends and family close? Why had He taken Paul from me just to leave me alone? Where was this new path? All I got was silence.

It was then that I decided to rise above my pain, my sorrow, and my self-imposed limitations. It was not until I started to make constructive changes in my life, for myself and by myself, that things really started to change. It had to start with a new attitude of gratitude. I had to stop thinking "impossible" and start thinking "I'm possible." I needed to rid myself of the old, negative, subconscious thinking that was keeping me imprisoned in my mind. It was time for a new me!

So, on faith, I quit my sixteen-year job waitressing at Denny's in December of 2020, radically changed my eating habits, and lost 50 lbs. I cut out processed foods, sugar, dairy, wheat, and at that time, meat as well. God wanted me empty so that He could fill me with something greater. He did not disappoint.

I put on my brave heart, sold my house and everything I owned within a three-week period, submitted my novel to Friesen Press, and moved to Mexico to continue writing. I found an enlightened community of like-minded souls. We helped each other heal the physical wounds and emotional traumas from our pasts. I am now pain-free for the first time in over forty years. Yes, God did keep his promise to me!

Since coming to Mexico in September of 2021, I channeled my second book within three months. I included the back history from *Peddlers* in my new book, *Havanna*. I submitted my novel in December of 2021 and thought that I was finished with the series. God had other plans.

The third book, *The Dreamspellers,* was given to me in a three-minute download in May of 2022. It took me six months to write it as I was busy creating a new life for myself. I have been so blessed to have a new outlook on life, a new body, a new attitude and lifestyle, and a slew of new friends. I have been growing in leaps and bounds.

Once I learned to fully love myself, everything changed. I started to honor and respect myself first and foremost. I now live in my integrity, in harmony with everything around me. I realized that my early connection with my sister had given me an understanding of how to be one with God, nature, and all living things.

My transformation has been a miracle! Am I perfect? No, but I continue to walk in the light that I could once only dream of attaining. God did truly have a mission for me, and once I got out of my own way, my life has become what God truly intends for all of us. We are meant to actualize our creative spirit in everything that we do. We are not humans having an odd spiritual experience; we are spirits having a human experience.

In finding my connection to Source, I also found my purpose and my passion. I dared to dream of a life of thriving, not just surviving. My life has taken off and expanded in ways I never thought possible. I look forward to many more years of bringing hope and spiritual insights to my fans through fictional stories.

Sarah Jane Worley

Digital Entrepreneur

https://www.linkedin.com/in/sarahjaneworley/
https://www.facebook.com/SJWParis
https://www.instagram.com/sarahjanewy
www.sarahjaneworley.com
https://msha.ke/sarahjanewy

Welcome Sister, Si-star, Mother, Daughter, Madame, Mademoiselle, Gypsy Queen, Spiritual Badass, Warrior Woman, Rock Star, Creatrix, Mystic Goddess.

Sarah Jane Worley is a solo parent from the UK living in Paris, France. With 20+ years of experience supporting lawyers and top executives in the corporate world, she was struggling in survival mode and deeply unfulfilled.

The patriarchal system is failing, and as we enter the age of Aquarius, women worldwide are awakening to our power.

As a high ticket affiliate marketer, Sarah empowers driven, self-responsible, action-taking women to find their voice, be authentically themselves, build a personal brand and monetize social media to unleash their full potential, create legacy wealth and impact in the world. The true magic lies in the transformation, becoming the best version of yourself, empowered to thrive and live a life you truly love.

I am honoured that you are here and thank you for reading my story.

RESILIENCE RISING: A WOMAN'S UNFORGETTABLE JOURNEY HOME

By Sarah Jane Worley

Our worth is not to be measured by the love a father withheld.

We are not to define our value by external factors. We are all inherently worthy. We find our worth when we look within. Self-love and recognizing self-worth is where transformation begins. Surround yourself with sisters and cheerleaders who fully support and celebrate you and your fully expressed self, for the Goddess that is you - you are worthy!

A wisp of hair trailed into my mouth as I chewed. Spitting air to remove the hair from my tongue, stubbornly, it remained.

I stood up, leaned forward, forced out my tongue, licked the bath towel, wiping and spitting until finally it disengaged and left my mouth.

Raising my right leg midway up the door to reach the door handle, then raising my right foot to lift the toilet seat, a shimmy dance shifting the transparent dress up just enough to reveal my naked arse to pee. The cistern flushed with a push from my big toe, and I wiped myself on the bath towel hanging over the side of the tub.

* * *

"Are you ok?" a voice said.

I lay outstretched like a frog, frozen.

I lifted up both arms, and suddenly felt intense pain surge up my body; my vocals let out a scream that bounced off the wall.

"FAAAARK!!!"

How did I get here?

PARIS

(*Phone ringing*)

"Do you want to move to Paris and come work for me?" asked my friend, John, a Partner in one of the largest law firms in the world.

"Fuck yeah!" bored with the commute and daily grind of London.

She had me, Paris. I fell in love with her deeply. The café culture, the intimacy of the jazz bars, strolling the left bank, my apartment on Île St Louis...

It's a cliché, but that certain *je ne sais quoi* cradled me in a familiar embrace, reassuring me this was where I belonged.

I celebrated New Year at the foot of the Eiffel Tower, lit up like a rocket ship, ignited for take-off as sparks rose up her frame, fireworks blasting left, right, and skyward. It was truly spectacular, yet by New Year standards, it fell flat. I was there alone.

My idealist self visualized strangers grouped together, embracing, holding hands, dancing like a collectively trained flash-mob crew, unified, rejoicing in recognition of unity, as we celebrated this monumental date—a new millennium.

In reality, drunken strangers banged into me as I walked through the crowd amidst the trash—strewn aftermath of the revelry, homeward bound.

Crossing Pont Louis-Philippe in the dark night sky, no one else was in sight at this hour. I looked down into the murky dark water wondering, *how long before Dad noticed anything had happened to me if I threw myself into the river Seine?*

I engaged with other expats, met some musicians, and made friends who came and went.

I joined a big band playing saxophone. Musicians always had weed to smoke—a habit I picked up when I first met **Him** in London. The hunt for a dealer at *Les Halles* no longer required.

* * *

Christmas was approaching, so I called Dad.

"Hi, what are you doing for Christmas?"

"We have the family coming over; no room at the table."

"Sorry, what?"

"What about me?"

"You're not family."

"WHAT?" I said, confused. "Are you trying to tell me something?"

"Yeah, there's no room for you!"

I slammed down the receiver.

I sat at the table with a group of expats, strangers, divorcees, misfits, and later, I sat alone in my flat eating an M&S Chicken Kiev.

SHATTERED GLASS

We almost lost Dad—an automotive design engineer working abroad—in a horrific car accident. I was nine years old. He was at the wheel of his beloved Jenson. A motorcyclist emerged from a side road, heading directly towards him. Dad swerved to the other side of the road to avoid collision. The motorcyclist followed suit, seemingly on a suicide mission, repeating the manoeuvre several times.

Mission accomplished.

When Michael and I arrived, Dad was out of the coma, sitting up in the accident ward. I'll never forget how the hospital smell stung my nostrils, nor visiting the wreckage, catching sight of the sheepskin Dad had been sitting on, drenched in dried blood, despite Mum's pleas of,

"Don't look."

Entering the ward, I searched for him; walking past the first patient, I noticed a young man had lost both legs from the knee down. Mum's presence at bedside was the only directive that it was Dad; face bloated, head shaved bald in readiness for cranial surgery. He was unrecognizable.

I requested the toilet and threw up in the bowl.

Surgeons opened him up from ear to ear, "or else a minor flu could have killed him," they said.

Dad was a handsome man before the accident. The facial injuries he sustained required metal plates inside his skull.

Despite being blind in one eye, Dad got back behind the wheel and resumed life with work, but something changed.

We ate dinner together as a family at the table and watched a lot of TV. Dad worked overseas for long stretches; he was emotionally unavailable when he was present. Being distant, disconnected, and disinterested was not his fault; the *Father Wound* runs deep in my ancestral lineage.

* * *

Mum's health had been compromised since an early hysterectomy removed cysts on her ovaries; an immediate double mastectomy removed the lump in her breast.

The cancer spread, and chemo went ahead. Mum lost all her hair and wore a wig.

The stairwell opened onto a wide corridor—Mum's profile was visible through the porthole window of the door, lying on a bed. I knew then that she had left her body.

I looked down the corridor to see medical staff announcing unthinkable news to Michael and Dad. Mum had a brain seizure. My heart was ripped out of my chest. She was 51 years young.

The deepest, most softly felt love, the *always-be-there-for-me love, I-can-count-on-you-no-matter-what love, here's-some-money-don't-tell-your-Dad* kind of love, the nucleus to our family, was no more, and life would *never ever* be the same.

Brother Michael, Dad, and I clung to each other like shipwrecked souls adrift in a stormy sea, desperately clutching a lifebuoy of comfort from our familiarity—as if letting go would plunge us into an abyss of overwhelming grief and tear us apart. It did.

The pain was immeasurable. The devastating winds of sorrow carried me forward in a zombie-like state.

Feeling desolate, numb, hollow inside, guilty even for breathing, I was desperate to find something to fill the gaping hole in my heart—this colossal void of losing my dear Mother had left.

* * *

Within a year, Dad met a widow with three kids, ending his daily disappearance upstairs with a large whisky shot.

"I hope you never know what it's like to feel lonely," he said.

Dad sold our family homes, upgraded his own, and took leave from our lives.

LONDON

"Get in."

An awkward silence, followed by an authoritarian command.

"Drop me here, thanks."

The car rolled on.

"Please stop the car," I said.

"No," he replied firmly.

"I want to get out," I affirmed, unknowingly about to embark on the ride of my life.

"Let me out," I repeated, mad at myself that I was even sitting there.

"Listen to me. This is how it's gonna go down. This is what you're going to do …"

I could feel the engine's power surge as the car picked up speed and the wheels gained momentum.

"Stop the car!" louder now, releasing the seatbelt security from my chest.

The car's headlights cast a warm glow on the road ahead.

"You're not getting out," he insisted, "until you …"

He wasn't backing down. Neither was I.

My right arm reached down for the hand brake and pulled. The car maintained speed as he kept his foot on the floor. He grabbed my arm off the hand brake to release it, returning his hand to the steering wheel as I grappled it again. His hand was back on mine, our fists entwined.

I reached for the hand brake again, then promptly gave a triple right hook to the side of his face. His hand was on my shoulder, forcing me to the far side of the seat.

"Go on then, get out!!"

A release button clicked the door open. The tarmac reached up to meet me, creating friction. I held on to the inner door handle like my life depended on it, my torso parallel to the chassis, dragging along for a stretch. My senses kicked in, I let go. Deceleration burned my skin. I came to a halt, and my body slumped at the roadside in the gutter, as the car continued on its way.

I lay there for a moment. In the following hours, I made my first statement to the Police.

They thought **He** was a stranger and that he had stolen my car. **He** was no stranger to me, and they couldn't have been more wrong.

DESIRE'S DECEPTIVE VEIL

(*Funk music playing - Bustin' Loose*)

"Hey, I've been looking for you!"

A tall, dark, handsome man stood before me.

"What? …all your life?" I replied in jest.

"Do you want to get out of here? Let's go to the Limelight."

I followed **him** through traffic in my Peugeot 205 Gti. We arrived at the club, and went straight in.

He was suave, alluring, and had the gift of the gab. I was beguiled, no, *bewitched*, discovering his world; a distraction from grief. I was so lost.

Pleasure and gratification were deep, daily, and our thirsts were insatiable. I had never met anyone like **Him**. It was exciting and new— a non-stop, lustful, passionate liaison. I felt so Alive.

He sensed my naive vulnerability.

I did a dumb-ass thing, allowing **him** to use my identity for some dodgy deal. I asked no questions and had no regard for myself. I had three mortgages in my name, and with Dad announcing the sale of our family home, I had nowhere to live. Reluctantly, **He** took me in. I became a voluntary prisoner in one of the houses.

I kept down a job, paid the mortgages when social housing payments weren't forthcoming, and maintained the facade of his HQ where we lived. Mind games, manipulation, many threats, blackmail, a brothel, and a fire...

* * *

The dawn raid's door smash woke me up to see armed Police at the foot of the bed. They cuffed and carted **him** off to Bellmarsh on criminal charges. A short stint on remand and **He** was out.

My own prison walls closed in, threatening to suffocate my soul.

A long narrow corridor, walls towering above me on either side like silent sentinels, held me in my vulnerability. I was down on the floor again.

I awoke finally, with an urgency to break free from this self-imposed confinement.

My oppressor had left. What was I waiting for?

Bombing down the motorway, remnants of my life in photos flying out the window onto the road, whipping up into the wind, and disappearing from the rear view.

A MOTHER'S ODYSSEY

Dad's words about loneliness echoed in my mind.

Alone, craving connection, I took up dating and ran several ads on Craigslist, as you do—offering a kaleidoscope of humanity—opulent realms of high-end luxury five stars, to the raw and gritty corners of a dive bar-liars, cheaters, don't-ask-don't-tell, underbelly of the Universe. Perfect!

I was 20 weeks pregnant when my son's Father returned to America, parting with promises to return for the birth. A friend was with me instead, diligently attempting to capture Raphaël's head crowning, eyes brimming with tears of *joy*, camera wobbling as she witnessed the miracle of birth.

Of course, I would choose a man that wouldn't be there for me, or his son. *Of course!!*

As a solo parent, I've been unemployed, flat-broke, and struggling with multiple failed businesses.

Fearful for our future, hopeful to inherit Dad's estate, I learned that *no one* owes you a damn thing in life, and that only *you* can save yourself.

* * *

In the depths of my being, I discovered an unusual inclination; an unconventional relationship with life's challenges.

I am a pain slut!

Others crumble under the weight of burdens. I found myself oddly invigorated by the struggle.

It's not that I enjoyed pain *per se*; not consciously. Rather, I found an unspoken pleasure in navigating life's difficulties; carrying a heavy load with resilience and determination, embracing the struggle as part of my *identity*.

The more I have faced, the stronger I have become.

I can do it, and I can do it all on my own—thank you very much!

In a world where help is available, I chose the solitary path, finding solace in the knowledge that I am self-reliant. The weight of financial struggle only added to my resolve.

Instead of succumbing to despair, I transformed my financial challenges into stepping stones, each hurdle a lesson in resourcefulness and creativity.

Despite my secret pleasure in navigating the stormy seas of life alone there were moments of exhaustion. As a single mother, days were demanding; nights were long. Yet, I never gave up. Struggle became a companion, a constant reminder of my tenacity and unyielding willpower.

Every trial was an opportunity; every setback was a chance to rise again. I have a quiet determination and an unshakable spirit.

I was never a victim of circumstance. I am a warrior, bravely facing the battle and finding my way; a testament to the strength of the human spirit; how one can find pleasure, not in pain—but triumphing over it.

One can carry a load with dignity and grace, and with it comes the unwavering belief that I can weather any storm that comes my way.

DOWN NOT OUT — REDEMPTION'S CLIMB

I learned that money has masculine energy, and my Dad "*never choosing me*" is deeply interlinked to my self-worth and a core reason why I never seemed to get ahead financially.

I dove into personal development. I learned the Five Love Languages. I based my own value and self-worth really low, and I would continue attracting avoidant, unavailable men like him, *my Father,* until I chose myself.

I went deeper into healing the *Father Wound,* beat the fuck out of feather pillows with a baseball bat, participated in sister circles, self-love practices, nervous system regulation, breathwork, Neurosomatic Attunement, Kundalini yoga, Qoya, ancestral healing, and online sisterhood for trauma healing and growth.

I knew that I had to forgive my younger self for the decisions I'd made, forgive **Him** for using and abusing me, and forgive my Father for abandoning me—for when you forgive others, you free yourself.

I decided to create a new story, to shift my identity, lifting me from a life of struggle and mediocrity into a life I love.

I learned how to heal my money blueprint, start manifesting, and transform my bank account.

* * *

Breaking both my elbows in a cycling accident was a profound initiation into receiving as I could do *nothing* for myself.

A long journey of healing.

Losing mobility in both arms was no accident. When you have steered off your soul path, life redirects you.

It is time for a course correction, connecting to my heart, my artistry, and what I desire to create in the world, my personal Legacy!

Life doesn't happen *to* you, it is happening *for* you.

Every time it has knocked me down, I get up.

This third strike down is my last!

I was Born to Rise—and Sister, so were you!

Dr. Stephanie Duguid

Do Good Leadership
Speaker

https://www.linkedin.com/in/stephanie-duguid/
https://www.facebook.com/groups/dogoodleadership
www.drstephanieduguid.com

Dr. Stephanie Duguid is a native Texan who was raised in a Christian home with a very loving, single mom who was a high school teacher, her biggest influence, and the typical Texas woman until her untimely tragic death in 2001. Dr. Stephanie found purpose and passion through the experience of losing her mom and mentor, working to find the positive light after a dark experience. Dr. Stephanie shifted her outlook from a tragic loss to a life of service, support, and empowering women in educational leadership.

As the founder of Do Good Leadership, Dr. Stephanie is a 30-year educator, professional speaker, leadership coach & mentor, and radio host who strives to help women become intentional and purposeful in reaching their full potential. She helps women in education develop positive leadership skills to become confident leaders. Reach out to connect or work with Dr. Stephanie today: www.drstephanieduguid.com

EMPOWERING WOMEN IN LEADERSHIP: DECIDE, DISCOVER, DEFY

By Dr. Stephanie Duguid

My story begins when I was a little girl. My parents got divorced when I was 6, and although I was very close to both parents (and still am with my dad), I lived full-time with my mom. My mom was a force of nature. She was the typical Texas woman…big hair, long nails, bright lipstick, high heels, and a big smile. She was a high school teacher for more than 40 years, a leader in the church, and worked with Habitat for Humanity.

As a high school teacher at Dulles High School in Stafford, TX, she was beloved by her students and other teachers alike. Students resonated with her. They absolutely loved her and kept in touch with her years after graduation. She would invite students with no place to go into our home. She would also find odd jobs for students to do around our home and in our neighborhood to help students in need have a way to earn an income. She just had a giver's heart full of service.

In the All Saints Episcopal Church in Stafford, TX, which happened to be across the street from Dulles High School, mom was a lay reader and chalice bearer in the church and was very involved. She loved being around other people and helping to support them in any way that she could during a service, in the choir, or during one of the camp experiences over the summer. Later in her career, Mom became involved in Habitat for Humanity. She simply loved helping others in the community. Although she wasn't very handy with tools, she was great with entertaining and would always make sure that people had what they needed at the job sites, and she did so with a huge smile on her face and in her heart.

My favorite thing about my mom was that she was the Welcome

Wagon lady in Sugar Land, TX. I have a picture of her actual Welcome Wagon graduation in 1977. If you are not familiar with Welcome Wagon, it was a way to connect people who were new to a community. When any new family moved into the community, my mother would go to their house, knock on their door, present a very bright smile and happy cheery face, and she would be invited into their home. Once inside she would simply start a conversation, ask several questions and interact with the new members of the community, making them feel welcome. She would offer a few goodies from the town out of her yellow wicker basket lined with plastic roses and give her contact information if they ever needed anything in the future. She knew how to communicate, build relationships, and make them last!

Mom was able to connect with everyone! She was a great model for leadership connection and communication. She could talk to anyone, young or old, student or legislator; she could simply connect. We would have these amazing conversations and we would talk about my future, education, where I would go, and what I would do. We'd also talk about career goals. My mom was really my mentor in all aspects of my life...and she had great practice. She taught government, economics, and leadership to high school seniors for 40 years.

In the fall of 2001, I started my first teaching job at Country Meadows Elementary School in Peoria, AZ. Mom did what she always did and sent a bouquet of flowers to celebrate my first teaching job. The day was so busy that I didn't stop to call and tell my mother thank you for the flowers. And unfortunately, I never had the opportunity to do so.

Suddenly on August 23rd, 2001, at the age of 61, she was gone. She was in a single-car accident where she fell asleep at the wheel. I was 27 years old, and I had just completed my third day of my first official junior high teaching job. When she died, I was lost! She was my mom, my friend, and as I mentioned, my mentor. She would guide me in all that I would do. I didn't understand why she was taken as she was one of the best people that I knew! I didn't think it was fair. She wasn't supposed to go! Not now!

And to make that time in my life a bit more challenging, do you remember what happened about two weeks later? That's right, 9/11 and the attacks on the United States. With all of the sadness, shock, and heartbreak, it was at that moment I knew. I knew why my mom had to leave this earth. I knew why she had to be taken.

Do you all remember that I said she was a Welcome Wagon lady in Sugar Land? Well, my take is that God needed my mom to be the Welcome Wagon lady for all those lives lost during the 9/11 attacks. That was my way of dealing with her loss. She always wanted to serve others and I feel that she is still serving even though she is gone.

Through this situation, I realized that I do not have control of everything in my life. I really cannot control anything. I was scared and full of self-doubt.

I then came to the realization that I only have control of myself. And that means that I am in control of my attitude, my thoughts, my outlook, my perspective, my mindset, my circle of influence, and my responses. When mom died, I could only see the negative aspects and felt that that would hold me back in my life since my mom, and mentor, was gone.

I did have my husband of three years who was an amazing support for me personally (and still is after 25 years). And I did still have my dad who I was close to. But my mom was my mentor.

But then I found hope in my own interpretation of her role after 9/11. She was needed by a higher power to help others to serve, something she had always done her entire life. So, I made the decision to follow her mission in life…I wanted to serve others.

That day I **DECIDED** to make a change in myself.

Now some might say, "Oh yeah YOU can just decide to make a change," but it is not that easy. I agree it is not that easy. From my background in health, wellness, and education I have come to understand and realize that if you're going to make a change in your life, nobody can tell you to make a change. You must decide for yourself. And once you decide, you can make that change. But to decide to change, you must be so uncomfortable with the situation that there is no other alternative but to make a change, think about it!

In my situation, my mother was gone, my mentor was gone, I was in a spiral, and then I found hope…I **DECIDED** to make a shift to move forward. I decided change had to happen.

So, if we try to make changes by ourselves, are we affirmed we are going to be successful? Not necessarily! To make a change, we need guidance, persistence, consistency, and accountability; we need a mentor.

After my mom died, I started searching for a mentor. Of course, at that time I didn't really have anyone at my work, or in my family. So, I looked through other methods online and found people like Tony Robbins. Tony and others had self-help books, videos, cassette tapes, and VHS tapes. I know I'm showing my age now! And although Tony Robbins is amazing, he wasn't the mentor for me.

All the mentors I found were men. Now, when we look at men's mentors, we see some specific characteristics. Many, not all, are very aggressive, specific, tell you what to do, and the communication is very sharp. Simply stated, very masculine.

But as a woman looking for opportunities for growth professionally and as a leader, I wanted a woman as my mentor, incorporating the feminine approach. My mom was no longer around, and I didn't have any other resources. So, I decided that **I CAN** do it! I decided to be my own mentor…again, no road map at the time. I had to figure it out myself.

As my own mentor, and even if I worked with another mentor, I had to **DISCOVER** who I was and what I wanted. I had to really reflect and ask myself what I wanted to do and why I wanted to do it. Of course, I had challenges, blocks, and detours. But along the way, I always had this **BELIEF** that I could do it.

You see, sometimes you just have to sit and be. We have to be still and take in everything that is around us while being honest with ourselves. That is the time that your body begins to wake up…that is confidence coming in, a new fire, and a new belief!

You see, discovery isn't a single question such as "Who am I?" It is being honest with yourself and with your responses at every marker in your journey. Was it easy? No! Was it quick? No! Was it necessary? Yes!

You see, I wanted to be a confident leader, but I had some fear! How could I be a leader? I was young. I was just getting in the profession. I was a teacher. But I wanted more…

Fast forward 15 years. I was then the Dean of Academic Instruction at a college. I now had the leadership "position" that I wanted, but not the leadership role I envisioned. See, many people hold a title, but they are not a leader at all. I wanted to be different; I wanted to be impactful, empowering, and to serve and support others. I wanted to DEFY the odds.

When you **DEFY**, you must acknowledge and celebrate; you must accept all you have done and claim it. You did it!

When I began my position as Dean of Academic Instruction, I came into a toxic environment. There was no united direction, no guidance, lots of negativity, policies were ignored, and a lot of complaining occurred. I was thinking, "Oh my goodness, is this what leadership is all about? Dealing with all the bad things?"

Have you ever been in a work environment where you just didn't like to go to work? That was this environment. But I knew I could help to make it better...I **DECIDED**. I knew I wanted to be a transformational leader; I wanted to find opportunities rather than focus on the problems.

My first big challenge was that I was a peer moving into a leadership position. I was now their leader. That transition alone was a challenge. So what was the opportunity?

I used it as a way to show I understood what they were experiencing; I understood the pains, struggles, processes, and procedures. I had to display my confidence in my abilities while helping colleagues go through a process of **DISCOVERY**.

But most importantly, I was their advocate! I was their voice. That first year was the most difficult, but also the most rewarding.

I created a vision for the division. A vision I shared over and over again. We also had a mantra: "Be Kind and Stay Positive." I also shared the **WHY** in everything we did. That made a world of difference.

I then made it a point to meet with each department leader on a monthly basis to let them share the pulse of their division—no hidden agenda on my part.

The most important part of all of the changes: consistency. And guess what? It worked. The entire academic division began to turn around. We were being positive, successful, impactful, and empowering others! I was able to **DEFY** the odds and be a transformational leader.

When we are faced with a challenge, a barrier, a roadblock, what do we do?

We question ourselves; We question our paths. We question our decisions. And now, more than ever, we see folks taking resistance as a sign to stop. We feel that life is supposed to be a straight line! We start at the beginning and ride along to the finish line with ease. No resistance! But life is actually full of sinkholes, lakes with no bridges, terrible storms, and boulders on the road. We tend to get pushed off our path often. So how do you stay on track?

If you are in education, what keeps you going back to the classroom, the office, or the college each day?

Your purpose…

What is your purpose? This is your strong sense of worth, the reason you get up each day. It is your lighthouse. It is something you are so passionate about, you will do anything for it. By knowing your purpose, you have a beacon to return to. However, many times we get lost and forget our purpose. The key is to keep it visible and return to it often.

Your purpose will be your roadmap to help you **DEFY** the odds!

Again, I started my journey when I was 27. I had to decide that I was going to make a change. While I was in K-12 as a teacher, athletic trainer, and even in higher education, I was on my path to discovery. I took in all the information from my experiences (good and bad) and found out what worked for me. And in the end, I defied the odds and became the academic leader I desired to be.

Now, I am a mentor to other women seeking positive leadership skills to become that confident leader.

And where did it all start? With my mom, my mentor, my guide. It all started with my belief in myself.

But in the end, it was all about **Decide, Discover, and Defy.**

So, on my journey, I realized that there are three overarching steps on a leadership journey that help develop positive leadership skills and confidence to become a leader. Those three steps are **Decide, Discover, and Defy.**

Know that you too can **Decide, Discover, and Defy.**

Decide: You must decide that you want to make a change, that you want to grow, and that where you are right now is so uncomfortable that you have got to do something different.

Discover: When you have decided to change you will need to discover your new purpose, vision, goals, and yourself. You will need to reflect, practice some introspection, and see where you need to adjust.

Defy: Be the one who defies the odds. Be the one who takes your future into your own hands; be the one who sets the example for others. Be the one who is confident, strong, and unstoppable!

YOU CAN BE AN EMPOWERING, POSITIVE, AND CONFIDENT LEADER!!!!

I invite you to become a part of my free community for women in education who want to become confident leaders. Let's connect today on FB @DoGoodLeadership.

If you are ready to Decide, Discover, and Defy and want to see if we are a good fit to work together, please reach out to me today! https://drstephanieduguid.systeme.io/metamorphosis

JOIN US AND BE PART OF
THE DREAM TO RISE FAMILY!

Do you dream of transforming your life, attracting more abundance, and becoming the best version of yourself? If you're ready to turn those aspirations into reality and create a life of impact, it's time to embark on an empowering journey with Dream to Rise.

Since its inception in September 2020, Dream to Rise LLC has been dedicated to guiding individuals through their struggles and helping them manifest their dreams. Our mission is to spread hope, love, and peace, and we do this through a variety of transformative services:

- Manifest Your Dream: A 12-week, one-on-one program tailored to help you design and live your dream life.
- Dream to Rise Inner Circle: Join our community for ongoing support and inspiration.
- Dream to Rise Podcast: Tune in for empowering conversations and insightful stories.
- Published Works: Explore my books like "My Journey Into Becoming" and the collaborative "Overcoming Self-Sabotage" and "Dream to Rise" anthology.
- Speaking Engagements: I share my message at various community events, international conferences, and annual meetings.

Sharing your story is a powerful way to illuminate the path for others. By doing so, you empower them to live their purpose and become their best selves.

Connect with Me, Cynthia Concordia

Website: Dream to Rise https://www.dreamtorise.info

Amazon Author's Page: Cynthia Concordia's Books

"MY JOURNEY INTO BECOMING":
https://www.amazon.com/dp/B09PP7XNLH

"OVERCOMING SELF-SABOTAGE":
https://www.amazon.com/dp/1960136089/

"DREAM TO RISE" ANTHOLOGY: Get your copy here:
https://dreamtorisecynthia.gr8.com/

Mastermind Group - Dream to Rise Inner Circle:
https://www.dreamtorise.info/so/4fN-hXGRm

Podcast - Dream to Rise on Apple Podcasts:
https://podcasts.apple.com/us/podcast/dream-to-rise/id1619091475

Social Media

Facebook: https://www.facebook.com/cynthia.concordia
LinkedIn: https://www.linkedin.com/in/cynthia-concordia-2b51b8116/
Instagram: https://www.instagram.com/cynthiaconcordia/
YouTube: https://www.youtube.com/@cynthiaconcordia8346/
TikTok: https://www.tiktok.com/@dreamtorise

A Special Request

If my book has inspired or helped you, I would be incredibly grateful for a short review on Amazon. Your feedback is invaluable to me, and it helps refine and enhance the message for others.

Thank you for your support and for being a part of this journey. Together, let's rise above our adversities and live our dreams!

Much love,
Cynthia Concordia

Milton Keynes UK
Ingram Content Group UK Ltd.
UKHW050743280324
440234UK00013B/222

9 781960 136336